"McNeill's series of 39 portraits (Ginsberg, amphetamine heads, drop is glorious, warming and humane.. tion, which reproduces all the sta drugs and the inner city, the calm (self, present as participator, whose courage and grace each ensuing crisis to its lowest common denominator, which is people. These columns stand as the truest translation between ourselves and the alien culture that emerged from our back yards and went into San Francisco and New York to be reborn. They affirm that generation gaps are bridged not through imitation... but through truth. For all those who pursued White Whales and yellow submarines, Don McNeill may be Ishmael.... A doubly lovely treasure."

—*The Washington Post*

"An excellent example of [participatory journalism] can be found in Don McNeill's *Moving Through Here,* a collection of fragile but timely tuned pieces by a *Village Voice* writer who was drowned in 1968. McNeill's reports on the hip, drug and flower-child scene of New York's Lower East Side were the work of a sensitive insider, seamlessley attached to the world he describes yet still able to be lucid and critical. They're 'feel' pieces rather than topical accounts of events; slight as they are, they have the transparency of good history and an unobtrusive rightness that makes them more impressive between covers than they were in the noisier pages of the paper. Though subjective in the best sense, they hardly need the first person: a living subject informs every detail, shapes each perception."

—Morris Dickstein, in *Gates of Eden*

"Cleanly drawn and finely detailed. McNeill brought a sense of awareness into harness with a reporter's compassion, and the result is unsensational, dispassionate, good journalism... good writing, no mistake about it."

—*Los Angeles Free Press*

"Like the quick brush sketches of Japanese artists, these pieces catch with uncommon immediacy the feel of their time and place. Don McNeill had an extraordinary sense for the truth of a moment and for the truth beyond the moment."

—*New York Times Book Review*

"Don McNeill saw and wrote so clearly in the short time he had that his work has illuminated not only that time but also reaches beyond."

—Nat Hentoff

"Don McNeill was the only reporter I ever knew who transcended his by-line... His pieces stand as small chunks of truth—too precise to be literary and too real to be journalistic."

—Richard Goldstein

"A magnificent achievement."

—Harrison Salisbury

"Don wrote the truth. And he kept getting better all the time. Those are the two best things I know how to say about a writer."

—Jack Newfield

"One of the finest reporters of the counterculture in which he took part was Don McNeill. [*Moving Through Here* is] one of the most necessary documents of the period. McNeill grasped the rapid transience of the scene, its opportunity for descent with the traditional hope of regenerative ascent, and its real danger within the invitation to live mythically."

—Eric Mottram, in *Blood on the Nash Ambassador*

MOVING THROUGH HERE

MOVING THROUGH HERE

by DON McNEILL

*Introductions by Todd Gitlin
and Allen Ginsberg*

Epilogue by Paul Williams

CITADEL PRESS
A Division of Carol Publishing Group
New York

CITADEL UN DERGROUND

First Citadel Underground Edition, June 1990

A Citadel Press Book
Published by Carol Publishing Group

Editorial Offices
600 Madison Avenue
New York, NY 10022

Sales & Distribution Offices
120 Enterprise Avenue
Secaucus, NJ 07094

In Canada: Musson Book Company
A division of General Publishing Co., Limited
Don Mills, Ontario

Manufactured in the United States of America
ISBN 0-8065-1165-6

To Dan Wolf, Editor of *The Village Voice:*

I ALWAYS KNEW IN MY HEART THAT I'D FIND
A NEWSPAPER TO LOVE, AND I'VE FOUND ONE.

This book is a selection of articles written by my son, Don McNeill, for the weekly newspaper, *The Village Voice*, in New York City, together with some pieces found in his personal papers. It is the story of a year, running roughly from the big beginning Be-In at Central Park in the spring of 1967 to the bloody Yip-In at Grand Central Station in March of 1968. It was a busy year for Don, a kind of break-over breathless year. And so it seemed this book best shaped itself of things most hastily written: on the night before the weekly deadline, typed in odd moments on half-sheets of paper, jotted down in his journals. Some day soon, he thought, there would be time for a careful book.

For me to thank all who helped put together what is here would be presumptuous, because what they did, they did for Don. But if names must be named, deep thanks go, of course, to Allen Ginsberg and Paul Williams, whose writings bracket Don's here like beautiful bookends; to his *Village Voice* family, past and present; to so many friends who came through at just the right moment, often unknowingly, with just what was needed; but most of all, perhaps, to Sophie Wilkins of Knopf, whose faith in the book Don so longed to write never faltered, even with his death.

Virginia Sims
October 9, 1969

CONTENTS

INTRODUCTION TO THE CITADEL
UNDERGROUND EDITION

Don McNeill was resident anthropologist of a tribe that was already lost during the year it was forming, the incandescent and scary 1967-68. A cultural civil war was opening up, which was partly a fight over turf—who would control the Haight-Ashbury or the Lower East Side—and partly a fight over labels. Although widely misunderstood as a generational set-to, it was closer to a confrontation of moral styles: hairy vs. smooth, you could call it; loose vs. up-tight; love vs. war; to borrow Philip Rahv's literary-historical term, redskin vs. paleface. Whatever you called it, something *weird* was emerging (revolt? subculture? lifestyle? tribe?). In the name of straight anxiety and surveillance, legions of journalists and other cultural tour-guides descended upon the weirdness, noting the long hair and the drugs and beads and beards, earnestly asking what *out of sight* meant, while those who were out of sight were quite covinced that if you had to ask what it meant, *you didn't get it, man.* Insiders and outsiders alike brandished their attitudes and blind spots like badges of identity.

McNeill, I sense, came to the weirdness without worrying whether he was an insider or an outsider. He didn't apply for a visa. He went to the hippie scenes because they touched him to the quick, they roused (as people said) his energies. When he got next to the tribe, he opened his eyes. He saw a scene thrashing around for a name and a way of understanding itself, and he wasn't too quick to stamp it. He learned as he went and reported what he learned as a series of exercises in learning. The closer he got to the mercurial scene, the more complicated it looked and the more it changed. The scene was an assemblage of microscenes transforming themselves, under pressure, at high speed. Prefab or either/or thinking didn't wear well. And quickly McNeill had to wonder whether the new world was already slipping away.

The strangeness of things was, needless to say, difficult to convey even then, in real time. Hirsute young people hurling flowers at the police! A grouplet called the True Light Beavers, passing out a handbill declaring "There are no problems, there are only things to be done," then promptly disbanding! What in the world was this? McNeill's disarming answer was: Well, just what it looks like. McNeill caught such moments in their own terms, turning the style of so-called objectivity to his own uses.

His statements were so plain, his literary manner so guileless, his art so understated, a casual reader could miss his delicacy of judgment, or the peculiar aptness of a sentence like "It is a lot of energy to deal with." His Quaker manner was to record strange goings-on as if they were not at all strange; he did not crash into the freak world and exclaim about it in a sort of psychedelic onomatopoeia, in the style of Tom Wolfe or Michael Herr. Rather, he seemed to meditate as he wrote, finding what Zen would call the suchness of things. Things, people, actions were promising, cavalier, wondrous, crazy, but there they were! look at that! and writing about them was a kind of discipline, a way of knowing.

McNeill had a gift for vignette, but I don't want to give the impression that he was nothing more than a miniaturist. The sociological riff in "The Runaways" is a cameo masterpiece, as in: "There has never been a generation so detached from their parents. All of the practical binds are gone. It has been decades since the average middle-class family needed their adolescent children for anything more than dish-washing, baby-sitting, and lawn-mowing. For the parents, the postwar ties were emotional ones; for the children, the ties were material. Now the children, by rejecting the parents' material values, also throw off the need of support. The society has reached such a point of affluence that a resourceful kid can live off its waste. A kid who lacks resources can live off his peers, who are, more often than not, willing to sustain him. Every commune carries a few."

"The Runaways," like other articles gathered in *Moving Through Here*, also catches one of McNeill's themes—the media as a drug and a political weapon, the eerie ways in which the ignorant and sensational and stagy press processed what they beheld. Like Richard Goldstein, also in *The Village Voice*, and Julius Lester in *The Guardian*, he saw that the vibration set up between the street and the spotlight was a mighty deforming force. "The 'Love People' and tribes are happening on the East side," he wrote, "but you won't find them under a glittering marquee. You won't find them through press releases or on network television. They're shy. Right now, the movement is like buds on a tree that's been through a long winter. And floodlights would kill the buds." They did. McNeill recorded that too.

High hopes, wide eyes, big talent: McNeill appreciated innocence, including his own—and only reporting which was true to that innocence could *get* the scene, take the measure of it. But McNeill was also that marvel, an honest witness; and as his writing (and the scene) proceeds, he doubts more, so that the book ends up reading like a quiet *Bildungsroman*. Abbie Hoffman and friends dig up a tree to plant on a dug-up piece of the Lower East Side. McNeill, pro-tree, pro-action, goes along for the ride, but he also follows up and reports that

the tree dies. This may seem a small thing. But McNeill is
also far from romantic about drugs, or the runaway life. He is
on to amphetamine danger, and early: not everything that
straight society says is *ipso facto* false. There is nothing
glamorous about the fifteen-year-old with the false ID who
said, "I've been here three days. Do you think I'll last a
month?" McNeill is absolutely, bravely clear-eyed about
white self-flagellation in the face of black power bravado,
including a speech by Black Panther Party chairman Bobby
Seale (pp. 215-17) which is must reading for those who want to
forget the sadomasochistic loops of racial politics during
those not exactly golden years.

And consider McNeill's report of the Grand Central Yip-In
of March 22, 1968. To write about police brutality in *The
Village Voice* was nothing special, and McNeill had the
advantage of his own bleeding head—two cops rammed him
into a glass door. But to criticize the recklessness of the
Yippie high command, without exculpating the cops or the
city administration, this was something remarkable. McNeill
wrote that the Yippies had led their people into a box canyon,
that the confrontation was "pointless." But in that wondrous
and dreadful year of God-seeking and assassination, when
millions of young people felt to one degree or another that
the old order was breaking down and they were going to
found a new one, and lines were drawn accordingly, honesty
had to overcome the sense of disloyalty, and often did not
(details available in Abe Peck's sensitive study of the tortured
career of honesty in the underground press, *Uncovering the
Sixties*).

McNeill ends his report on the Grand Central showdown
with the words: "somehow it seemed to be a prophecy of
Chicago." Those words hang there. McNeill died in a
swimming accident two weeks before the Democratic Convention began in Chicago and the Domecratic Party exposed
itself as feeble and brutal at once, with consequences that are
still working themselves out. A '60s voice would say there was

something *cosmic* about McNeill dying that way, just as a lot of innocence was about to die. I prefer to think that what was cosmic was the plain absurdity of his death, just then, at age twenty-three—an absurdity McNeill would have appreciated.

Possibly he would have though it droll, too, that (as I have just discovered) I am finishing this introduction on what would have been his forty-fifth birthday. *Far Out.*

Almost from the start, McNeill was elegiacal about the hip scene, and one inevitably wonders what he would have made of later developments—the women's movement, thousands of communes, the gay sensibility, Charles Manson, the Weathermen, cocaine, the parade of swamis across the land, punk, Soho, the club scene, crack, skinheads, the fragmentation of rock, Ronald Reagan, Donald Trump, people living in subway stations.... Whatever he would have been doing at forty-five, he (along with the vast majority of movement veterans) wouldn't have been running a networking business on Wall Street. Or pushing antiquarian "Sixties" shtick.

Twenty years on, the striking thing about McNeill's tone is how receptive it is without being stupid or mean-spirited. Much of what passes for avant-garde culture today has become infinitely more knowing—and brittle, and spiteful, and studied. This is not just true in the slicks. Today's *Village Voice* too often oozes a knowingness so thoroughgoing, so savvy, it makes cynicism look radiant by comparison. But who knows what subterranean chords might be tuning up, in what tunnels? Hard as it may be to believe, things happen outside the media glare, even today.

Astonishingly, everything Don McNeill describes in these pages took place in a single year. Perhaps the breakneck pace helped writers like Don McNeill flourish, coaxed the best out of them. The prevailing sense of the unreal made fiction difficult—since fiction, whatever its devices for expressing the weird, presupposes some bedrock reality that stays put—and made journalism take wings. Since then, history in the

American side of the round world has decelerated—how could it not have? But nothing stops, and nothing stops the young from growing up young, and the young in every time and place have their particular ways of being ill-at-ease, bitter, innocent. There are new tribes, new traps, new styles for the thrill and difficulty of being young. They await their explorers and anthropologists, their political organizers, their journalists.

Todd Gitlin
Berkeley, California
December 21, 1989

Todd Gitlin is the author of *The Sixties: Years of Hope, Days of Rage* (Bantam), and *The Whole World Is Watching* (University of California Press), among other books. He is a professor of sociology at the University of California, Berkeley.

McNEILL'S MEMORY

A chronicle of events each unique, beginning w/ inauguration of LSD(League of Spiritual Discovery)NY Ashram now defunct, thence on Easter Sunday Central Park Be-In 1967 details alas more imprecise than poetry this reporting, the late sweet-tempered Don McNeill's posthumous book recalls failed societies, transient underground symbols and slogans from Flower Power to Armed Love, fugitive Street-Theater garbage acts and banana electricities, temporary social effort poems the Free Stores & apocalyptic ecologic hippie cityblock Sweep-Ins, Persons (Whitman's word) appearing on Lower East Side and Haight-Ashbury, heat phases & deathly speed tendencies, Zen Hindu American fads & heroic-accomplished syncretisms, cloud drift of Commune gatherings in the Eastern urb, beat plebean visions note the Serenos robbed of tenement peace monies by Pentagon phantoms, Tompkins Park's yesteryear History's mass busts and fearful free concert breakthroughs, Abbie Hoffman emerging prophetic burning dollarbills on Wall Street's balcony & planting trees on St. Mark's Place, or recycling carbon-soot back

on Con Ed Power slaves' pants-laps, new drugs manifest-
ing dated like STP in spacetime decade speedup.

Though sorry there's general gossip about myself,
shamed to make conscious this book thru which I flit by
hindsight idealized ineffectual, I'm glad some newspaper
glimpse of Herbert Huncke's "guilded gossip" remains, &
Amerindian prophetics were recorded for millennial aye,
& that these Street Theater Reviews're mind-filed for
reference by fresh-memoried highschool revolutionaries
who'll want account of recent Holy Art Planet Society experiments. McNeill was also gracious to report young
underground hopes & works to middle-classy sensitives,
newspaper elders & *Village Voice* bohemians thus fairly
forewarned by him what ways New York Chicago kids
contra armed police this decade are the exact Prague children that confronted Soviet-uniformed armed police hu-
mans. This prophecy Merlin shall make, for I am the King
of May.

After that prophetic armed police riot in Grand Central
Station whereat he reports his own head shoved through
doorway plateglass by a uniformed paid agent of the State,
and as the cry *"Vengeance on the murderers of Jacques de
Molay!"* rose horrific on St. Mark's Place, the author died
oddly, drowned in a leafy pond near Woodstock town. I
knew sir McNeill as a tender fellow, smiling psycho-
political secretary, Buddhist naturalist & light-minded
planet inhabitant matured, who when new-dead seemed
to've unburdened himself of the worldly drag our Police
State scene'd become, & calm-hearted shaken off his
material life like dewy water.

Allen Ginsberg
September 30, 1969

PART ONE

Manhattan as a stage . . .
a red velvet curtain at the Jersey entrance to the Holland Tunnel . . .
with a fanfare of horns the curtain opens and the actors and
audience enter as one, to begin

THE LONG MARCH IN A CIRCLE!!!!

being a week-long caravan around Manhattan in ever-decreasing
concentric circles until it disappears down a rabbit hole in the dead-
eye center of Central Park

day and night, fending off foes, binding wounds, carrying casualties,
stopping to eat, with a canary-colored cart for supplies (& a horse?),
with banners & square flags & round flags & triangular flags, and
music (fife & drums) & flutes & tambourines, getting pretty scroungy,
window-shopping, garbage-picking, eating chocolate bars for
energy, scouts (Tonto), lookouts, packs on backs (scout knives),
sleeping on the street around a camp fire hydrant, canteens, Harlem,
ceremony, celebrations, dedications, lots of plaques (George
Metensky slept here), lots of bells, cook stew in the back of the
cart, candle lanterns at night, mirrors, tent to ball in, masks, props,
pray for Indians, what about one-way streets?

DISCOVER NEW YORK! Stick a flag in the ground & do the thing
& set out to explore it. Pass your house on the 4th day. Daniel
Boone pales before such temptation. Civilize Manhattan and
colonize Brooklyn, & Queens. Bronx blocks the bridges & defends
the moat. What lies beyond the Hudson?

This is our second chance.

OPENING IN THE WEST

ASHRAM ON HUDSON STREET

The setting was West, two blocks from the river on Hudson Street, but the inclination was definitely East. With a host of folk heroes present, an informal house-warming of the League for Spiritual Discovery's Manhattan headquarters also became the initial meeting of a conspiracy designed to introduce some San Francisco ecstasy to grim New York.

The LSD Center, still under construction after weeks of expensive delays, is in a corner storefront at the unlikely location of Hudson and Perry streets. Mandalas and a poster-sized portrait of Timothy Leary are taped to the windows below the ornate sign that identifies the place. Inside, the walls and ceiling glow with abundantly patterned, paint-chipped pressed tin. The cement floors are covered with carpets. Books and handicrafts fill low, makeshift tables toward the front of the store, an area which will become an office and "decompression chamber" to prepare for entering the meditation room in the back. Candles are lit, the air is pungent with incense, and a chilling draft penetrates the room.

The Center was warm that February night, due to the body temperatures of the hundred people who filled the place. They had come to enjoy a rare meeting of the Triumvirate. Richard Alpert and Ralph Metzner were there. Leary was about to land at JFK Airport. The air in the Center was foggy with the smoke of cigarettes and incense, illuminated by the lights of BBC cameras. The congregation was turned on and passive, and Metzner rose to tune them in.

"Let us begin," he said, "by meditating quietly for a while to find the calm center. I suggest that you sit in some position so that your spine is straight, and concentrate on your breathing." The audience shifted and straightened, some crossing and some cramping their legs into a lotus position. Some were at ease, an ascetic ease with the back erect and the eyes blank. Others were uneasy and restless, shifting and restless, and were relieved when Alpert stood up.

"Now that you've found some calm center, I would like you to try and meditate on this. On Monday I had breakfast with Allen Ginsberg and Marshall McLuhan in Toronto. Allen said that the only valid criticism he knew of LSD was by Krishna Murti, who said that LSD involves choice and the goal is a choiceless awareness." Alpert sat down and the audience tried again.

Metzner and Alpert had just returned from San Francisco, still glowing after the proof of the monumental Be-In of early January. Alpert rose, relaxed, to speak about the recent changes in San Francisco's Haight-Ashbury community. Ten thousand hippies constitute a potent political force, Alpert explained, and the psychedelic storekeepers are becoming wealthy. "The community has to learn how to deal with success," he said, "and they are confronting a lot of issues that confront any ashram." ("Ashram," an important word, is defined by Ginsberg as a "self-sufficient community formed around the teachings of a particular guru.") The biggest problem of an ashram is its tendency to split up.

In San Francisco, storeowners are incorporating, Diggers are screwing up the system by giving everything away, and many are splitting for the mountains. "Ken Kesey is out looking at ghost towns," Alpert said, "and, if they find one, Kesey could become mayor, Neal Cassady sheriff, and the Merry Pranksters the City Council."

Earlier, Leary had called from JFK Airport; Nina Graboi, director of the LSD Center, spoke to him on the telephone, then quietly spoke to Susan Leary, sitting nearby, and announced to the group that he was coming. Now Leary had arrived, grinning but silent.

The front door of the Center opens. Allen Ginsberg, Peter Orlovsky, Gregory Corso, and a tall, thin, bespectacled man walk in. William Burroughs is recognized in seconds. Alpert simultaneously cracks, "He looks so straight." They laugh as Burroughs and Ginsberg pick their way through bodies to the head of the room, and sit on the floor. Alpert continues.

"My trip is very simple," he said, fondling a peacock feather. "I'm trying to be like the sun and warm everybody around: cops, hippies, teeny-boppers, Sidney Cohen." Alpert had the peacock feather in his teeth, and was gently swaying it up and down. He proposed a "spiritual rebirth" on the first day of spring. "Secret groups could go out at night and paint buildings." Walter Bowart wanted to paint the blacktop in Tompkins Square Park, he related. Mayor John Lindsay and Parks Commissioner Thomas P. F. Hoving said that he could chalk the sidewalks, but not paint them. "You can leave all the dirt on the Lower East Side," Alpert predicted. "You can found a spiritual community around the dirt."

Ginsberg mused about the pragmatic aspects of an ecstatic revolution in New York. A meeting like the Be-In, "an apolitical pow-wow in the style of the American Indian," is a lot of work, he explained. The Haight-Ashbury scene is "a structured organization without a single head but with lots of competent 'heads.' I imagine that it could happen here, but somebody has got to do it. I'm not going to."

Ginsberg continued, and Orlovsky rapped loudly in reply from the back of the room. Orlovsky was in prime form, and the interruptions were comic and gross. "Here we don't have anything like the Fillmore," Ginsberg said. "We have the Dom, but that hasn't developed into a sacramental meeting place."

"You can't have anything up there because it's a goddamned lonely place," Orlovsky broke in. "It's full of green." Laughter. "He takes speed," someone said. "I'm off it now, folks, just take vitamins," he rapped back. Roars of laughter and, with a flurry of parting words, Orlovsky walked out. He crossed the street and began to polish the family Volkswagen bus.

The discussion continued, pondering possibilities of a tribal scene in New York. "A peaceable manifestation of everyone young should happen at the UN," Ginsberg mused. Murmurs of agreement. "The UN is beautiful," breathed a girl. "The New York police can't touch you," another rejoiced. Someone suggested a street-cleaning celebration on the Lower East Side. "I'm not ready to go out and clean up mattresses in empty lots," Ginsberg said, bringing them down. "But I would if everyone else would." And they were relieved.

It was close to midnight when the heroes began to leave, and the people slowly strayed off. The discussion evolved into conversation and the LSD housewarming-conspiracy was over.

THE BE-IN WAS THE BEGINNING

As the dawn sun gleamed off a backdrop of molded metal skyscrapers on Easter Sunday, a medieval pageant began in the middle of Manhattan. Laden with daffodils, ecstatic in vibrant costumes and painted faces, troupes of hippies gathered on a hill overlooking Central Park's Sheep Meadow to Be-In. By sunset, ten thousand celebrants swarmed in great rushes across the meadow, and thousands more were dispersed throughout the rest of the park. Bonfires burned on the hills, their smoke mixing with bright balloons among the barren trees and high, high above kites wafted in the air. Rhythms and music and mantras from all corners of the meadow echoed in exquisite harmony, and thousands of lovers vibrated into the night. It was miraculous.

It was a feast for the senses: the beauty of the colors, clothes, and shrines, the sounds and the rhythms, at once familiar, the smell of flowers and frankincense, the taste of jellybeans. But the spirit of the Be-In penetrated beneath the senses, deep into instincts. The Be-In was tuned—in time—to past echoes and future premonitions. Layers of inhibitions were peeled away and, for many, love and laughter became suddenly fresh.

People climbed into trees and made animal calls, and were answered by calls from other trees. Two men stripped naked, and were gently persuaded to reclothe as the police appeared. Herds of people rushed together from encampments on the hills to converge en masse on the great mud of the meadow. They joined hands to form great circles, hundreds of yards in diameter, and broke to hurtle to the center in a joyous, crushing, multiembracing pigpile. Chains of people careened through the crowds at full run. Their energy seemed inexhaustible.

The password was "LOVE" and it was sung, chanted, painted across foreheads, and spelled out on costumes. A tall man, his face painted white, wearing a silk top hat adorned with straw flowers, wandered ethereally through the Be-In holding aloft a tiny sign reading "LOVE."

The costumes ranged from Easter Parade hats and morning suits to high-mod gear to psychedelic robes. Many people painted their faces in wild designs and colors ranging from chalk white to glowing lavender. They often included a dot, a tiny mirror, or a diffraction disk pasted on the forehead. One man was dressed in a suit of long, shaggy strips of paper. Another wore a jacket covered with buttons, all upside down. "This isn't a day for slogans," he explained.

Although hippies dominated the Be-In, it was by no means exclusively a psychedelic event. Many families came to join the Be-In after the Easter Parade down Fifth

Avenue. Be-In posters in Spanish invited members of the Puerto Rican community. Grandmothers and executives, hippies and housewives mingled together in harmony. Three nuns appeared wearing Be-In buttons.

A young boy, a Negro, was skeptical about the hippies. He turned to his father. "But, Daddy," he said, "they look so funny."

"You shouldn't say that," his father admonished, "until you know them."

The posters for the Be-In said "BRING PICNIC," and anonymous press releases urged people to bring flowers, food, and Easter eggs to share. The main activity of the day was giving. Most of the flowers and decorated eggs were passed around many times. Sticks of incense, smooth pebbles, sandwiches, and jellybeans were offered among the crowd. You could yell, "Does anyone have a cigarette?" and get one in seconds.

The Be-In had no center of activity. The action continually shifted from point to point, from group to group and, from a high point in the meadow, you could watch the surges of people to the peaks of activity, usually closely followed by a tribe of people extolling the newly discovered banana high. A herd would converge on a spot and, in seconds, you could hear the chorus of the banana mantra—"Banana, Banana"—and see a large, wooden, slightly phallic banana bobbing in the air. You could almost always see the banana out of the corner of the eye, aloft in a tree or rushing through the meadow. At one point, the banana clan, consisting of about fifteen people, surged to the northwest, converging, with a full-throated banana chorus, on the refreshment stand for a coffee break.

The event was at once surreal and beautifully absurd.

Three girls wandered through the crowd of thousands, one of them holding up a key chain. "Did anybody lose some keys?" they droned. "Anybody lose some keys to a Volkswagen?" The girls wound in and out of the groups of people, all around the Sheep Meadow, impossibly patient, holding up the keys.

The Police and Parks departments quietly and unofficially cooperated with the Be-Ins. A police car arrived shortly before seven in the morning, and the few hundred people already gathered rushed the car and pelted it with flowers, yelling, "Daffodil Power." The police, astonished and covered with flowers, beat a hasty retreat.

Throughout the day, a few police watched the Be-In from the edge of the Sheep Meadow. They made no arrests. When police approached the two men who had stripped off their clothes, hundreds rushed and surrounded a group of five cops, alternately chanting, "We love cops" and "Turn on cops." They crushed tighter and tighter. The banana hovered overhead, and the police had no escape. The chant switched to "Back Up, Back Up" and, just in time, the people peeled off the cops.

A few thousand were still encamped on the hill, dark except for the flickering light of a few fires, when the police arrived in force around 7:30 p.m. Police beamed lights on the hill and used bullhorns to order the Be-In to disperse. Again the crowd rushed the cops. This time it was more tense, moving toward a nightmarish showdown. Then it eased, and the police let them stay, watching the crowd from a distance. The Be-In broke up shortly afterward.

"The police were beautiful," said Jim Fouratt, who helped to organize the Be-In. "It was really strange and it freaked them out, but they were beautiful."

The four main organizers of the Be-In were Fouratt, an actor; Paul Williams, editor of *Crawdaddy* magazine; Susan Hartnett, head of a group called Experiments in Art and Technology; and Claudio Badal, a poet-playwright from Chile. With a last-minute budget of $250.00 they printed 3,000 posters in English and Spanish, and 40,000 small notices in a Day-glo design donated by Peter Max. The posters appeared on walls and telephone poles in every part of the City. The notices were tacked on doors, stuffed in mailboxes, and passed out on the street.

"We tried to remain anonymous," Fouratt explained. "People would ask who was organizing it, and we would give them a Be-In button and tell them, 'You are!'"

Fouratt doesn't think that a Be-In can succeed or fail. "It just is," he said. Nevertheless, most participants thought that the Easter Be-In was a triumph. It avoided many of the pitfalls of the first Be-In, a "Gathering of the Tribes" in San Francisco's Golden Gate Park earlier in the year. Personalities dominated the first Be-In, and the activity was centered on a stage. The New York event seemed more spontaneous.

Another Be-In has been scheduled in conjunction with the Spring Mobilization to End the War in Vietnam, but some people are skeptical about mixing Be-Ins with politics. The Be-In seems almost a sacred event, harking back to medieval pageants, gypsy gatherings, or the great pow-wows of the American Indians. At the same time it is a new and futuristic experience which, once refined, offers great promise. But it should be refined carefully. It is a lot of energy to deal with.

3RD STREET SCRUB

The big yellow garbage truck rounded the corner at First Avenue and 3rd Street. Mercifully, the garbage men were prepared for the shock. Third Street was clogged with hundreds of hippies pushing brooms. The pavement foamed with detergent and clouds of cleanser filled the air. Third Street was getting a bath.

The driver shifted into reverse, but it was too late. Hippies swarmed to scrub the truck. They climbed onto the hood and over the cab with brooms and mops and buckets of water. The garbage man rolled up his window and the wash began.

The Sweep-In on Saturday was a success because it was a goof. Hippies had discovered before that it was safe to "Love." At the Easter Be-In, they surrounded cops, chanting "Love" and pelting them with daffodils. It worked: the cops were bewildered. At the Sweep-In, they discovered that cleaning was just as effective.

A cop walked up. A hippie began to scrub his badge. The cop had to smile.

They climbed streetpoles and scrubbed the groovy glass of the stoplights while the lights flashed red and green in their faces. They painted manhole covers gold and fire hydrants silver. Like locusts, they swept into basements and vacant lots and picked them clean of a decade's compost.

A young father, his child strapped to his back like a papoose, walked down 7th Street with a scrub brush and a stool. At each "No Parking" sign he stopped, climbed on the stool, and scrubbed the sign clean.

The Sweep-In, an idea kindled on Bob Fass's late-night talk show on WBAI, was originally intended for 7th Street. According to Fass, the idea embarrassed the Department of Sanitation. "They made a wild attempt to subvert it," he said. "They hit 7th Street four times the day before." Fass then contacted the Sanitation Department and established an uneasy truce.

Since 7th Street was sparkling, the Sweep-In was switched to 3rd Street. Many sweepers were unaware of the change, however, and throughout the day kids with brooms roamed through the grime of the Lower East Side looking for where it was "in" to sweep.

The first thrust hit 3rd Street between First and Second Avenues around noon. Trucks of donated Ajax cleanser arrived, and the soap was passed out to hippies, housewives, and a few Bowery refugees who panhandled the cleanser around the corner for a dime.

They shook the cleanser on 3rd Street, and pushed it around with brooms. Huge Sanitation water trucks arrived, first to wet the street and then to rinse it. Passing cars, stalled by the crowds, also got an enthusiastic scrub. Some drivers later complained that the cleanser damaged the finish.

The most enticing action was on the sidewalks. Much like the Be-In, participants passed out lunch, daffodils, incense, and chanted the glory of the now-near-sacred banana. They also took pictures of each other. Every third person seemed to have a camera.

After an hour, the Sweep-In dispersed to find a more

challenging mess. Cleaning parties seemed to concentrate on vacant lots and backyards, the traditional dumps of the East Side, perhaps in the hope that the ground could be salvaged for a vest-pocket park.

No dirt was immune. Even basements and hallways, where insulted superintendents resisted to no avail, got the Sweep-In treatment. The basements yielded moldy treasures. "I'm sure they found some sewing machines out of Jacob Riis photos," Fass commented. "The last time these basements were cleaned was in 1941 during the government scrap drive."

They cracked the gate to an ancient vacant lot on 3rd Street near Avenue D. A herd of hippies descended on the lot and began to gather the garbage, a foot-thick layer of bedspring, tin-can compost. Some swept in vain, others moved the refuse to the curb with hands, shovels, and buckets. They were silent in their determination. The only sound was the picking of the shovels and a solo drone of the now-familiar "Hare Krishna" mantra, accompanied by fingerbells.

In an hour, the lot was clean. On the curb lay a ton of garbage, carefully laden with banana peels and sticks of fuming incense. The lot was a pasture of hard, naked dirt. On the wall of the adjoining tenement, someone had painted "BECAUSE WE LOVE."

The lot, of course, was private property. The next day the gates were locked. In another vacant lot, on East 4th Street, the cleaning crusade went a bit further and tore down the fence. The next day, neighborhood kids used the area as a playground.

At five in the afternoon, a party began on 7th Street between Avenues C and D. It's a hippie block—an outpost in the Far East—and stereos blasted Beatles from the windows and onlookers hung from the fire escapes. A six-story banner, "FROM SUPER CARL—WELCOME TO 7TH STREET," honored a benevolent superintendent. Another banner, "LOVE, RELIGION OF GOD," was strung across the street.

At the end of the day, the City moved in. Garbage trucks came around to pick up the heaps of garbage on the curbs. Mayor Lindsay was delighted about the Sweep-In and praised it in his weekly report on WNYC. The Department of Sanitation was pleased and relieved. "We're very happy," a spokesman cooed, "when citizens of New York get involved in helping the Department keep the City clean and beautiful."

He may have missed the point. The Sweep-In was a glorious goof, but you have to sweep every day to "Keep Fun City Stronger than Dirt."

LIMITS OF FLOWER POWER

Saturday was Flower Power Day. It was a nice picnic but a lousy protest.

The theme of the peace demonstration was survival. After the fall of the Flower Brigade at the Patriots' Day parade the preceding weekend, there were fears that Flower Power Day might be a rout on the scale of the Children's Crusade.

But the turnout for the Armed Forces Day parade was

light, and the police escort was formidable, and the
Flower Power people survived intact.

Flower Power Day was one of a series of attempts by
the Committee for Non-Violent Action (CNVA) and the
Workshop in Non-Violence (WIN) to bring the hippies
into the peace camp. The handbills, printed several weeks
before, made the protest look like a Be-In. After the
violence on Patriots' Day, the peace people had second
thoughts. At a tense strategy meeting Wednesday night at
CNVA headquarters, it was decided that a confrontation
with the parade might be disastrous for the new recruits.
Plans to "zap the military with love" were abandoned,
and it was decided that the protest would remain in the
park.

After the meeting, CNVA and WIN seemed to abdicate
their sponsorship of the event. Neither the police nor the
press nor the Parks Department were informed about
changes in the plans. Saturday morning, three hundred
people responded to the handbill and gathered on the
lawn near Delacorte Theatre in Central Park.

They sat around on the grass and sang Dylan songs and
carried flowers and wore gentle buttons. They passed out
incense and talked to the television cameras, and ran
through the trees, keeping a weather eye out for guerrillas
from Fifth Avenue. It was a low-key protest.

Around noon, Allen Solomonow, a CNVA organizer,
suggested that those people interested in confronting the
parade get together. A meeting formed and they discussed the prospects of martyrdom.

"I have a suggestion on how to demonstrate Flower
Power," a girl said. She put an iris between her teeth and
held up her fists. "This is Flower Power," she said. "Your
hands are free."

A young, solemn man declared that he planned to sit in the path of the parade. "I've never been to jail before," he said. "I'd like someone to join me." No one did. He sat alone in front of the Metropolitan Museum as West Point cadets led the march down Fifth Avenue. Police took him into custody.

The message of the march was submerged in nonsense. CNVA had originally planned to send a delegation to place flowers on a war memorial near Fifth Avenue. Now Solomonow suggested that they march instead to the statue of Alice in Wonderland. "We're going to bless Alice," he said.

"I think you're carrying non-violence to absurdity," Paul Krassner commented.

"Now let's all join hands," Solomonow said as the meeting ended.

"How are you going to join hands," a voice from the crowd asked, "if everybody's holding flowers?"

The meeting disintegrated, and a deputy inspector approached Solomonow and inquired about a park permit. CNVA had not bothered to apply for one. Solomonow protested loudly, and a crowd gathered. Solomonow disclaimed leadership, and said the meeting was like a Be-In. The police threatened a summons. "Then you must give everyone a summons," Solomonow replied coolly.

The cop relented. "So you had a non-meeting," he said, smiling. "The next time you don't have a meeting, get a park permit."

Around two in the afternoon, the Flower Power people began a meandering walk toward the Alice in Wonderland statue. Mounted police followed the crowd as they wandered across meadows and through groves of trees. They arrived at the statue and swarmed over it. The police arrived and disentangled them, issuing a summons to one demonstrator who refused to disembark. Rookie cops formed a cordon around the statue.

Leaving Alice behind covered with mangled irises, the Flower Power people marched on to their Fifth Avenue fate. Police closed ranks as they approached the 72nd Street entrance to the park, and funneled the marchers onto the sidewalk. Escorted by a heavy police guard, they walked north to 78th Street through a light crowd of parade spectators. They stationed themselves opposite the Duke Mansion and, in lieu of protest signs, held their flowers aloft as the parade approached.

As the parade progressed, the love decreased. While formations from the Army, Navy, and Marine Corps marched by, the Flower Power people chanted, "Hell, no, we won't go." As mounted squadrons passed, many demonstrators screamed their protests. The horses, startled, bucked, and the men reined them in. As a squadron of Marines marched by, the chant was a ghoulish sing-song: "We know where you're going."

They "zapped the military," but not with love.

There were few incidents of violence. A middle-aged man, screaming "Kill the bastards," slugged Martin Jezer, a CNVA worker. Jezer emerged with his mouth bleeding. The man was quickly subdued and arrested by the police.

As the parade ended and the demonstrators began to move back to the park, two hostile youths forced their way through the crowd and began swinging. A dozen police lunged toward the brawl. As they shoved the marchers out of the way, some protested, shouting, "Police brutality." The peace-march beat turned out to be a thankless job.

The demonstrators then returned to the park and

headed for the Sheep Meadow to be-in in earnest. Love returned with relief and they paused to dance around the Bethesda Fountain and stopped in a tunnel to sing "Hare Krishna" and listen to the echo. As the Flower Power people sunned themselves in the Sheep Meadow in the later afternoon, the Armed Forces Day parade and the war in Vietnam seemed far, far away.

MEANWHILE, TO THE EAST

THE EAST VILLAGE

It's better to call it the Ninth Precinct. The boundaries are the same: from Broadway to the East River, from 14th Street to Houston. But you can't ignore the bulk of the Lower East Side, which extends far below Houston Street, nor the reality of a slum by calling it the East Village. It's the Ninth Precinct. Perhaps the only thing in common to all those stark blocks is the number on the doors of the police cars which patrol the streets.

Otherwise, it must be one of the most diverse neighborhoods in the world. Its origin has been a series of ethnic and cultural transfusions. Of each, pieces remain: the kosher delicatessens, the exotic fruits of the *bodegas* and the magic potions of the *botánicas,* the Ukrainian stores where families exchange raincoats and Easter eggs across the Iron Curtain, the frustrated Carusos at the fruit stands, and the glimmering windows of a *pasticceria* around a holy day. Grandmothers remain, because of other grandmothers, and each day they pack the benches in Tompkins Square Park like bleachers at a major league game. Only the game is over, so they relive it in conversation.

Unlike the West Village, in the spring of 1967 the East Side was almost exclusively residential, which meant that unless the tourist was invited inside, there wasn't much he could do except hunt hippies and shop for psychedelic souvenirs. Until recently the roster included only a number of boutiques, several bookstores, a few restaurants, and a lone discothèque. But that didn't seem to discourage the tourists. As the young rushed to join the hippie ranks, their elders flocked to observe, and the sightseeing buses came in caravans.

It is residential because people live in homes stacked upon homes, in block after block of fading tenements, which were inferior when they were built in the last century and which, needless to say, have not improved. Behind the often majestic façades, carved when immigrant labor was cheap and plentiful, are thousands of identical apartments, complete with a bathtub in the kitchen, which may be home for $62.50 a month, more or less. An inside bathroom is a luxury on the Lower East Side. The cockroaches are free.

Pablo, a tribal store at the grimy end of Bleecker Street, captured the essence of the area in a series of postcards. The photographs, by Philip Stiles, were in black and white. There isn't much color on the Lower East Side. Even the red brick of some tenements has been dulled by coatings of soot. For all the flower children, there aren't many flowers. The Lower East Side has the bleak air of postwar Europe, of industrial Manchester, with the tall 14th Street Con Edison stacks spewing dark smoke for a backdrop. Here, of all places, the hippies chose to make their home.

The pioneers were a scattering of beats and students, who forged the trail from the West Village in search of nothing more glamorous than cheap rent. This they found and, with it, each other. There was a camaraderie in the early 1960's, when Stanley's and the Old Reliable were frontier bars and amphetamine was available almost over the counter, and mad poets roamed the streets. It was sort of a secret, kept secure because nobody really cared. But as West Village rents continued to soar, the less affluent followed the path of least resistance, and soon St. Mark's Place became civilized, in the West Side sense of the word, and boutiques began to blossom next to *bodegas.*

The rents kept pace as the Lower East Side quickly evolved from a typical slum to a neighborhood with some subtle status. As the West Village grew sober with middle age, its kid brother to the east offered enticing alternatives. As off-Broadway productions began to be featured in the theater pages of the *Times,* maverick workshops and café theaters came to life in basements and storefronts across the East Side, fighting for survival against harassment by the City, and daring critics to disdain their work. Disdain they did, and out of the outrage came off-off-Broadway.

Some people came to the readings at the Café Metro and St. Mark's-in-the-Bouwerie for the poetry, and others came for the heat. Or they might have huddled around the radiator in Ed Sander's Peace Eye Bookstore, an outpost on East 10th Street, when their apartments grew cold on an icy winter night. Sanders might have been in the back room, printing the latest issue of *Fuck You/A Magazine of the Arts* on his rickety mimeograph machine. Allen Ginsberg might have stopped by on the way to his apartment down the street, past Avenue C. Or it might have

been the night when the Fugs first came together, when
Tuli Kupferberg stumbled downstairs from his apartment
next door to meet Ken Weaver and Steve Weber who
together set out to sing about the "slum goddess from the
Lower East Side."

The hippies arrived long before the label. At least there
were kids with long hair and a passive manner who
smoked grass and got stoned on acid and felt free in the
sanctuary of a slum. But when the label came, they were
ready to respond. On October 6, 1966, the day the California LSD laws came into effect, a group of colorful kids
came together in Tompkins Square Park. "Love," the
pink handbill read, "A Psychedelic Celebration." They
had flowers and incense and children and paisley flags
and they sang HARE KRISHNA HARE KRISHNA KRISHNA
KRISHNA HARE HARE with an old Swami who had recently
arrived from India. Maybe it was a catalyst.

That's when they became the hippies, and the local
press began to take note of each subtle shift in the emerging culture. The kids responded with vigor, even holding
press conferences. But some responded with horror, splitting for the country, or withdrawing into as much anonymity as shoulder-length hair and a necklace of bells
allow. With an eye cocked toward their sister community
in Haight-Ashbury, the lost children of the Lower East
Side began to organize their Eden. Soon there was a bail
fund to free busted brothers, and then came the tribes
and then the tribal councils. At the same time, enterprising young merchants began to open storefronts that had
been dead for decades. A year later, Peck & Peck, a
tweedy midtown department store, would advertise that
their special customer is the sort of woman "who carries
maps of Sumatra and the East Village in her purse." Still,

when she came to shop on St. Mark's Place she wore her cloth coat. Furs don't fit in the Ninth Precinct.

I remember the street scenes.

The Suckmobile, a vehicle which could only belong to the Group Image, hurtles down Second Avenue, ablaze with STP stickers. A stoplight interferes. Group Image Freaks, as members of the tribe are affectionately known, pour out of the back of the truck to dance in the intersection. The light turns green, they jump back in, and the Suckmobile goes off and away.

Gem's Spa at midnight, or at dawn, or at any time of the day. The sidewalk seems to run through the candy store at the corner of St. Mark's Place and Second Avenue. By virtue of its location, twenty-four-hour vigil, and survival stock of tobacco, Bambu papers, and egg creams, it is the official oasis of the East Village. A routine siren sounds and the candy store empties. "Good-bye," the guy behind the counter sneers. "They always split when the sirens sound."

A pimpled kid is standing on a corner waiting for the light to change. In his right hand he's clutching a brown paper bag, and he's twitching. He's twitching—and waiting for the light—because he has a kilo of grass in the paper bag. He is a dealer, an underground merchant whose stock is as essential to the East Side as salt was to the pioneers. And when he's delivering he doesn't jaywalk. Still, he debates the question: perhaps he would be less obvious if he crossed on the red light.

Every block has a different attitude, from the intimate to the intimidating. Every stoop has a shadow at night, every streetlight a glare. You tread between the two, a tightrope which is typical of the struggle for survival in the slums. It is night. The Ukrainian grandmothers are asleep and the Puerto Rican fathers may be getting off the swing shift. The hippie may be getting up, or going to bed, or walking in the streets in the middle of his day. Time is something he left behind.

The famous and the friendless: Andy Warhol, pale under the glaring lights in Ratner's, posed at a table with his flaming entourage. Outside, on the street, the perennial panhandler who has forgotten his own face. When a clean window threatens to remind him, he turns away, to spare himself.

The glamour and the gloom: the opening night of the Electric Circus, and St. Mark's Place is jammed with spectators to watch the big names enter the big tent. Bobby Kennedy, who is chairman of the benefit's committee, doesn't show, but George Plimpton does, and the opening is considered a success. The Electric Circus is launched as the biggest new business to enter an area chosen as a testing ground for the war on poverty. Within a radius of five blocks are more than ten antipoverty projects, teaching tenants how to go on rent strike to rid themselves of rats.

The Ninth Precinct is nothing if not diverse.

It is an island of social, political, and cultural experiment in a city where routine is a religion. It is a place to go to earn your stripes. And it is a place to go when you've lost them. For the hippie it may be a looking glass. For the country, it may be a mirror.

BED AND BOARD ON THE
LOWER EAST SIDE

Hippies are not as dependent upon parents' bank-books as *The New Yorker* cartoons would have you believe. When the psychiatrist gives up, when they take another acid trip or go back to their East Village lovers amid the final fury of a father's threats, when finally the precious monetary lifeline to home is cut, the offspring is not necessarily doomed to reconciliation or a job. He can, and often does, return to his East Side refuge to live and trip and screw, and he can count on shelter and sustenance. The new Bohemia, a mores-shattering society, has provided for victims of the Establishment. There is a well-carved niche in the structure for transients.

The word "transient," amplified by "Bohemia," brings visions of early Bob Dylan tromping down a daybreak MacDougal Street in the snow, after a huddling night of steam-heated coffeehouses. Or the vagabond image, hitching the truck-stop route to the Coast. But the East Village is another scene, and not quite as pretty. The kick is no longer experience per se. The theme has changed to the mélange of escaping, soul-searching, and discovering thyself: a difficult, agonizing process whether on an acid trip or an analyst's couch. It's not a story to tell your grandchildren.

His name is Fred. He is nineteen, and from Long Island. One year of college, enrolled for sporadic night courses at New York University, lives with a chick from Connecticut on Avenue B, and takes a lot of drugs. He flunks out of night school. Parents threaten to disown him unless he transfers to a small, Methodist college. His parents disown him, and the rent money disappears. Chick leaves, and after six weeks he gets evicted, and his furniture is in the street. He unloads all he can and, with three cardboard cartons of portable possessions, goes to visit a friend indefinitely. He will occasionally move, staying with a circle of perhaps ten friends. The three cartons are reduced to a shopping bag, their contents spread through ten apartments. He has no apartment, few possessions, sporadic money, and no obvious way out. Nor has he a job. He does have a place to sleep, food to eat and, somehow, drugs when he wants them. He is a ward of the scene, and he gradually becomes accustomed to it.

There is some distance, and some evolution, between the Establishment break and the transient commitment. It may have a number of eviction scenes, a huge debt for the telephone and gas, or perhaps more engulfing incidents like a drug arrest, or the necessity of being a confessed drug user in exchange for a draft deferment. With each stage, the road back to middle-class serenity becomes longer and more cluttered. And, with the almost universal self-fascination in this isolated society, values change. Privacy, for example, is easily sacrificed, material possessions become less important, clean sheets forgotten. Yet the body is sustained and the mind is at work circumnavigating the answer.

The transient rut is not a creative one. It is a fertilizing, pre-creative experience for a few. It is an interim for a few. For more, it is a long road down, laced with drugs,

especially amphetamine. Many dig the descent; oblivion
can be seductive. There is a fascination in being strung
out for days on amphetamine, a fascination in Rolling
Stones echoes, a fascination in the communal chaos of the
Lower East Side, as far removed from Westchester as is
India. If you wade in too deep, you may learn that the
East Side undertow is no myth.

It is an intensely personal quest and, in spite of
crowded apartments, very often a lonely one. "Sometimes
it's lonely," said a veteran transient. "Not like feeling
alone but like not understanding what's happening."
There are emphatic individuals beneath the easy stereotype, but, especially to the hosts, the stereotype often
manifests itself. The refrigerator is empty sooner, the clutter more obvious, and the quarters close, although most
East Side apartments are well designed for sleeping, with
floors covered with mattresses, cushions from discarded
sofas, and rugs. The action and the company are satisfy-
ing for a while, and the need is appreciated. Most hosts
can stay calm for a couple of weeks. Some hosts concede
to a colony. Groups of ten people in one apartment are
not unusual. Sometimes it becomes a narrow line between
the host and the homeless and, in cobwebs of sublets and
promised rent, an apartment may become a transient do-
main and the original host eventually forgotten. Possessions continue to dwindle. You tend to leave with less
than you came with, and the apartments involved become
a melting pot of personal trinkets. Some transients scatter
good intentionally. "It's something I like to do," said a
folksinger from Bucks County. "You take something and
leave it at the next place. It's a link."

The transient life seems to run in a cycle, and it often
doesn't end before a few bounces off the bottom. Someone

may live an hour-to-hour, night-to-night existence for six months. By then, his feet may be caught in the undertow. He has successfully escaped from the time-bound Establishment, and probably replaced it with the timeless world of the amphetamines and psychedelics. In time, however, he may wear out the welcome of his circle of friends, and feel the bottom coming up fast.

But the thing about hippies that *New Yorker* cartoonists don't seem to realize is their resilience. The East Village rope has a long end. In the summer there are rooftops to sleep on; in the winter, an occasional vacant apartment. Some apartments are empty and unlocked, explained an ex-amphetamine head, and they are "handy places to fall down, sit around in for a while, and scuffle through old magazines." But eventually it may come to the street.

Al, a young but ageless A-head, lives on a 9th Street block. It's just his block. He knows a lot of people on it and most of the day and most of the night he sits on one of the stoops. His connection is on the block, and familiar faces are good for fifty cents, good for a visit, but not good for a bed because Al is supposed to steal. Only small things. He tirelessly tries to start conversations. He always looks cold. Al has lived on 9th Street for four months.

It's easier for a chick to find a place to stay. Susan is nineteen. She went to Goddard for a semester and quit to come to New York. She has taken a lot of LSD and has been shooting amphetamine twice a day for six months. She is small, with dark hair, and was frightened when she knocked on the door of a strange apartment. She moved in, and didn't talk for days, and sat awake all night. The fellow occupants—three couples—were gentle, and she began to talk, but she still doesn't talk much.

Al was poor to begin with. Susan is a missing person, as are a lot of the transients. The East Side escape can be agony for parents, and many try to surrender the battle. Transient hippies are hard to find, to which "All is forgiven, Mom and Dad" newspaper ads are testament. The East Village is a general delivery kind of a neighborhood, and it can easily absorb a runaway.

The end, especially of the transient cycle, depends on the individual. Some enjoy eternal hospitality, avoid the drug-oblivion undercurrent, and dig the transient life. They will re-enlist. Some, sick and hungry and weary of roaches, call it quits and make some amends with the Establishment. And some descend even more, to a junkie-ghostlike state, to a hospital, to a car trunk. The rope often unravels before it ends.

HOME IS BITTERSWEET

A curious group of people gather at night in the Lower East Side *bodega*. They all live on the same blocks, wall to wall in the same tenements. They share the grime of the neighborhood, the garbage in the streets, the inescapable fear of a slum at night. They are there to buy different things; some not to buy at all. An old Puerto Rican woman sits in the *bodega* until it closes. Her face is lined with age, her cheeks hollow. She doesn't move her head, but her eyes follow you around the store, watching, recording each can you take off the shelf. She is there because she has no heat. It is winter and the *bodega* is the warmest place on the East Side.

A young man, also Puerto Rican, just off swing shift, buys canned pork and beans, beer, and cigarettes. Three kids dressed in Levis, boots, and heavy surplus-store jackets, buy soda, soup, bread, and a holy candle. The man at the counter is quickly bilingual, but happier in Spanish. He adds up the groceries on the bag and spreads out the change on the counter. The meeting is over. Everyone involved will go home over the same dark streets of the Ninth Precinct, where the cops walk in pairs. The man will go home to his family. The kids may go home to their families the next weekend, on Long Island. They are just on the East Side for a while, which makes it easier to take. The man and his family may be there longer. All of them will be glad to leave.

They are worlds apart, the hippie and the Puerto Rican. Add other worlds and other blocks on the East Side, the trim, stark Ukrainian neighborhood just west of Tompkins Square, the dwindling congregations of tiny synagogues. The hippies are unique in that they borrow freely from all the other cultures. They may buy groceries at the supermarket, bread at the kosher bakery, late-night soda at the *bodega*. And, to the bewilderment of their neighbors, the hippies contribute a culture of their own to the scene. Starting with ominous dress and long hair, and extending to stores for books, beads, and psychedelic props, boutiques are opening in long-vacant storefronts— all on the same streets, alternating in the same apartments. The worlds continually overlap without touching.

Bohemia has flourished on the East Side. The rents are

low, leases loose, the neighbors apathetic. You can furnish your apartment from the street Wednesday night, when furniture left over from an eviction is put out for the Thursday morning garbage pickup. You see a lot of sofas on Wednesday night—all without cushions. The cushions, portable and comfortable, are the first things to go.

The hippie and the Puerto Rican were the last to arrive. The older neighborhoods, west of Avenue A, are harder to move into, and the cheap apartments are now east of Tompkins Square. The Far East is a neighborhood of newcomers, and the atmosphere is tense, dissatisfied, with an air of betrayal. Few people arrive on the East Side expecting the smell of urine in the hall, or a view of a backyard filled with garbage.

The relatively small area has many facets. Each day it seems to go through a cycle. In the morning, shortly after dawn, Avenue C is an echo of a turn-of-the-century market street, pushcarts lining the curbs selling vegetables, shopkeepers stacking their wares around their doors, immigrant housewives shopping as their grandmothers did, their bread from the bakery, their meat from the butcher, their vegetables bartered from one of the many carts. All viewed through the early-morning haze which seems to last all day.

In the afternoon, St. Mark's Place begins to open. The hippie stores cater to an afternoon clientele, more still to a night one, and at night the street begins to swing. The core of energy on St. Mark's at night seems to exude from the crowds around whatever's happening upstairs at the Dom, currently called the Balloon Farm. Whether it is a psychedelic Trips Festival, or a Warhol megalo-spectacular, it attracts the tourists who fill the streets.

St. Mark's Place is otherwise lined with old townhouses

and struggling trees and, like the row of houses facing the north side of Tompkins Square Park, it is prime real estate and the rents have soared. Each block on the Lower East Side has a status, each area a reputation, generally declining as you get farther east. Aside from a scattering of brownstones, the tenement is the rule on the Lower East Side. Blocks and blocks of soot and stone walkups, the exteriors often elaborate, with friezes and gargoyles, and the interiors identical. The front door opens into the kitchen.

The new Bohemia can take credit for recognizing the incredible variety of possibilities in the tenement apartment. Basically, the tenement flat appears to be one of the most boring living areas ever designed by man. Into this dilemma hippies introduced the aerial bed—a platform and mattress midway to the ceiling, fur rugs, double-life-size photoposters of Bogart in *Casablanca* and Valentino as the Sheik, and, of highest priority, a media setup comparable if not exceeding those in their suburban homeland. A stereo is part of the survival kit. The cost of such a transformation is low; imagination is down-payment. Cover the windows, bolt the police lock, and forget you're on the Lower East Side—unless you hear noises on the fire escape, or your toilet is down the hall, or you're dying for a cigarette at 3 a.m.

An apartment can be covered up, with rugs and posters. The enthusiastic may attack it head on. Red-brick walls may lie behind a lot of plaster. Occasionally a fireplace. Or you can sand down the floor and stain the planks. Behind the bolted doors lie some beautiful apartments. But you still have to get home at night.

"I feel safe until I get past the park," a dark-haired girl said. "But the block between B and C is horrible.

Then I walk fast." Neighborhoods are judged at night.

And night is the worst part of the Lower East Side. Night is when you lock the door and hold the fort. If you want to go anywhere, you'll have a hard time. Cabs avoid the Lower East Side. The bus is infrequent. If hunger strikes, Second Avenue may be a long walk. If you live near Avenue D, you may settle for a trip to the *bodega*.

MAKING PEACE AT THE PEACE EYE BOOKSTORE

The fading "STRICTLY KOSHER" sign, a leftover from the days when the Peace Eye Bookstore was a chicken market, was gone with the front window. Gone too was the "Pot Is Fun" sandwich board that Allen Ginsberg had worn in the first LeMar demonstrations. And the rickety old mimeograph in the back room, which had turned out fourteen issues of *Fuck You/A Magazine of the Arts,* had finally been junked. It had been a rough winter for the little mags.

But Tuesday night, like a molting phoenix rising from the garbage at 383 East 10th Street, the Peace Eye opened again.

Perhaps one hundred people responded to the mimeographed invitations sent by poet, Fug, and Peace Eye proprietor Ed Sanders, and came to see the opening exhibit of literary artifacts which adorned the bookstore's subway-tile walls. Everything, Sanders insisted, was for sale: a six- by ten-foot banner used in the shooting of Sanders's epic film *Mongolian Clusterfuck,* Ken Weaver's certificate of undesirable discharge from the Air Force, a framed collection of pubic hair plucked from sixteen leading poets, and two much-heralded cold cream jars reputed to have been used by Allen Ginsberg. The cold cream jars went for $35.00 to an anonymous collector.

Friends and fans and Fugs wandered through the exhibit, which included all the back issues of *Fuck You,* a wall of little mags from d. a. levy * in Cleveland, who is now fighting obscenity charges, and the prosecution evidence from Sanders's own obscenity trial, from which he emerged victorious several weeks ago.

Anything could happen at the Peace Eye. Someone brought five pounds of raw hamburger in a plastic bag, to sell at a bargain price of $2.00. Steve Weber, a folksinger and former Fug, opened the bag, sniffed the hamburger, and bought it on the spot. "I'll take it home to the old lady," he said.

All evening firecrackers had been exploding up and down the block. But it wasn't until nine when the first one came through the door. Sanders closed the door, and a rain of firecrackers began. The Peace Eye was under siege.

A patron tried to leave. He opened the door, and was driven back inside by a hail of ladyfingers. Through a

---

* d. a. levy—young Cleveland poet and visionary mimeo magazine publisher (*MARIJUANA REVIEW*—"Do not smoke the *Marijuana Review*"), whose books were seized at Cleveland's Asphodel Bookshop by municipal Narcotics Squad raid, whose person was seized on charge of corrupting morals of a minor after reading aloud teen-age poet's pro-black power verse at coffeeshop, whose friends were busted and harassed as he defended his literary scene with legal vigor—finally committed suicide in 1968.—A.G.

crack in the door, they pleaded with the kids. "He's got to go home. He's got to get to work." Still the explosions continued.

So Allen Ginsberg went outside to make peace.

He ran out to the curb and began to sing mantras with great gusto, clashing his fingerbells. The kids were dumfounded. At first they gaped at him, but soon began to taunt, and more firecrackers flew at the poet's feet. Ginsberg kneeled in the gutter, in the grease between the parked cars, and kept singing. The kids glared at him.

"What are you afraid of?" Ginsberg asked.

"Why don't you go back where you came from?" a kid demanded.

"I live on the block," Ginsberg said, and kept singing.

The exchange went on for ten minutes, Ginsberg singing, kids taunting, firecrackers exploding from every side and Puerto Rican families watching, astounded, from nearby stoops. And then a kid started to sing with the poet, and Ginsberg would leap to his feet, and show the kid how to hold in his stomach, and then he was back on his knees, singing again, asking more questions, singing "Om Raksa Raksa Hum Hum Hum Phat Svaha!" And now the kid was clashing the fingerbells, and you could hear the mantras up and down 10th Street.

After twenty minutes, the firecrackers had stopped, and Ginsberg and the kid were sitting on the stoop next to the Peace Eye, still singing, with a smiling audience of thirty Puerto Ricans and poets passing around beer. And the kids who had been throwing the firecrackers were inside the store sweeping up the shrapnel.

And the Peace Eye was peaceful again.

ABOLAFIA FOR PRESIDENT

Louis Abolafia has balls, even if he does hide them with his hat.

A campaign flyer, showing the Presidential candidate naked except for a derby over his crotch, proclaims the campaign slogan: "What have I got to hide?" At the close of his "Cosmic Love-In," which ran for five days last week at the Village Theatre, his question may be answered.

Abolafia, a professional self-publicist who has made a career of fame-gaining schemes from hunger strikes to a gubernatorial campaign, decided early in 1967 to run for President. He opened up campaign headquarters in a tiny storefront on East 4th Street. He printed handbills, sent out press releases, and began an appeal for volunteers and contributions.

The campaign was slow to take off. A few volunteers appeared with hand-lettered signs at underground gatherings like the Easter Be-In. Abolafia, who can be charming, appeared occasionally on radio talk shows. But his big break was yet to come.

A few months ago, the Drigelgold Corporation purchased the Village Theatre on Second Avenue. Impressed with the success of the Fillmore Auditorium in San Francisco, the buyers hoped to turn the old vaudeville house into a similar profitable community center. When Abolafia approached them with promises of publicity, the theater was vacant and they agreed to let him stage a one-day "Love-In" for the cost of the lighting. Now Abolafia had what he always needed: a free stage.

He began to court the press in earnest, badgering columnists and grinding out press releases. He covered the East Side with posters and handbills promoting the event. The handbills listed a star-studded cast: Allen Ginsberg, Timothy Leary, Eric Anderson, the Blues Project, the Velvet Underground, USCO, Richie Havens, Paul Krassner, the Children of Paradise, the Free Spirits, and Swami Bhaktivedanta. With such a cast, the $3.50 admission (later reduced to $2.00 and finally to $1.00) was a bargain. But few of the stars ever appeared. "When some people drop names," Gregory Corso commented, "they bounce."

What the "Cosmic Love-In" did have was a profusion of unknown poets reading their work, a visual background of uncoordinated slides, films, and cartoons, a table in the lobby selling Abolafia posters and buttons, and occasional music. The Children of Paradise and the Free Spirits both made brief appearances. The Group Image played for two nights. "We needed a place to practice," one of them explained.

The audience—heavy with kids from the outer boroughs and Jersey who were attracted by the promotion—was disappointed by the absence of superstars. Louie blamed it on fate. On Wednesday he was still optimistic. "I saw Ginsberg at the Be-In, and he said he'd come. Leary has a standing invitation to drop in."

By Saturday, however, Abolafia had regrets. "Leary regretted he couldn't come down, but he's with me. He'll be in the next show. . . . Ginsberg is in town. He's out of

his head. He's tired. He's been on a speaking tour. . . .
The Blues Project have been recording, and are having
trouble coming down. . . . Richie Havens copped out not
because he wanted to but because he was out all week.
. . . Charlotte Moorman is supposed to come down tonight yet." Eric Anderson was at a concert in Virginia,
and the Velvet Underground was in Cannes with "The
Chelsea Girls."

Up until the last night, hand-made posters in front of
the theater promised the superstars.

But the "Cosmic Love-In" was by no means a failure.
The promises had lured the press. A crackpot Presidential
campaign, complete with hippies, superstars, bananas,
and big names, is good copy. The event was colorful and
Abolafia was quotable. The press came in droves.

Abolafia is media-mad. He counts columns and quotes
Nielsen ratings (twelve on the Allen Burke Show) with
Johnsonian fervor. He was delirious about the coverage.
The "Love-In," complete with photos, was featured in the
Times, the *Daily News,* and the old *World-Journal-Trib-
une.*

The Village Theatre extended the "Love-In" through
Saturday.

I asked Abolafia about his recent appearance on the
Allen Burke Show. "Allen Burke?" He took a deep breath.
"I was on the Allen Burke Show a year ago when I was on
my eighteen-day hunger strike. I got five columns in the
Herald Tribune. I've been on the Joe Pyne Show twelve
or fourteen times. I've been interviewed by the Russians,
by CBC, BBC, by the English press. A Norwegian reporter was here. The South American press has been here.
CBS is doing a documentary on me.

"Otto Preminger came down to see me," he continued.

"He called me his President." Blown-up photos of Abolafia with Preminger were taped to the literature table, alongside news clippings and announcement of his Johnny Carson Show. Louis Abolafia is not a modest man.

"I'm the center of the great cultural revolution in this country," he told Allen Burke.

"You're an egomaniac," Burke replied.

He bills himself as an artist, a poet, a philosopher. He claims credit for all the recent successes on the East Side. "I've helped organize the Be-Ins, the Sweep-Ins, the tribal rites. I was on WBAI helping to promote the March-In, uh, the March."

Abolafia is supremely confident when it comes to his campaign. "Bobby Kennedy doesn't have the college kids. I have them. I expect at least five to ten million votes from the aware people in this country. This is a whole power source that hasn't been tapped at all, and should be utilized. There are another forty million people in this country who never vote, and we hope to get them." He is not in the least concerned by the fact that he falls ten years short of the minimum age for the Presidency. The campaign is as phony as a nickel bag of oregano.

Abolafia is Goldwater-candid except when it comes to specifics about crowds and cash. I asked him how many people had come to the "Love-In."

"Oh," he mused, "like it's in and out, in and out, in and out."

I asked him how many tickets had been sold.

"Oh, I have no idea," he said. "We gave away hundreds. We gave them out in the streets. We wanted everybody to come. And I've been letting many people in free."

It was Saturday night and the first six rows of the 2,500-seat theater were filled. Other people were loosely scattered throughout the first floor of the theatre, some wandered in the lobby. There could not have been more than four hundred in the theater.

I walked out to the box office and asked the lady behind the window how many tickets she had sold that night. "Oh, a few hundred," she said. Two or three hundred? "Oh, yes," she said. "Definitely. At least."

An usher is permanently stationed at the door to direct people to the box office. Inside the "Love-In," a herd of cute teeny-boppers armed with bread baskets solicited contributions for Louie's campaign. "I have hundreds and hundreds of hostesses from all over the city," Abolafia said, "who come in and help out."

While I spoke with the candidate, three came up to turn over baskets of small change. He seemed embarrassed. "It's printing money," he explained. "Just enough to keep up expenses."

Most benefits expound their attendance and their take. And campaigns are required by law to present an audit of expenses and contributions. Abolafia has done neither.

Louis Abolafia is cool and charming and has a fair share of charisma. He cuts a dashing figure in his Zorro cape. He knows the catch phrases. When he talks about "love," the kids identify with their own concept of "love" and flock around him. And when the kids flock around him, the press thinks he's "where it's at." He's not, but the game has been working.

The "Love People" and the tribes are happening on the East Side, but you won't find them under a glittering marquee. You won't find them through press releases or on network television. They're shy. Right now, the movement is like buds on a tree that's been through a long winter. And floodlights would kill the buds.

DRUGS, DEALERS, AND DREAMS

GREEN GROWS THE GRASS ON THE LOWER EAST SIDE

He is twenty, a graduate of a suburban high school and a suburban adolescence. He has had some college, but dropped out to join his fellow middle-class expatriates in the East Village. He has split with his parents, is unemployed, wakes up in the afternoon, and lives in relative affluence. What's his line?

His line, very possibly, is dealing psychedelic drugs. By his trade, he plays a unique role in this fledgling society. He is the link between the underground and the underworld.

He is an obvious contrast to the traditional "pusher" stereotype, hardly the dirty old man handing out reefers in the schoolyard. Yet it would be a mistake to picture the dealer as Andy Hardy on the Lower East Side. He may be college material from a well-to-do home, who wouldn't dream of snatching a purse, but he is constantly engaging in highly illegal acts, felonies which could lead, under Federal and State law, to a prison term through middle age. The irony doesn't escape the dealer. "It's something to write home to Mother about," said a youth from Connecticut after a successful exchange.

There is also a contrast to the actual "pusher" situation. Whereas the average retailer of heroin is working to support his own addiction, the dealer in psychedelic drugs is working primarily for profit. Although most dealers themselves use the drugs they sell, the pot habit is neither as demanding nor as expensive to maintain as heroin addiction. Federal and State legislation severely distinguishes between a heroin addict selling drugs to support his habit, and a nonaddicted person selling heroin for profit. The latter is labeled the more "heinous" crime.

The profit motive is great. You can buy a pound of marijuana, sell it by ounces, and end up with three times the original investment. The profit remains as tempting at every stage of dealing—probably around six exchanges from field to joint. There are no hours, no office, no ties. It's an easy way to make a living.

There also seems to be a psychological motive. The dealer commands a certain mystique in the East Village. He is playing a far more dangerous game than the consumer, and he is respected for it. For himself, the excitement surrounding a "big deal" and the ritual and accoutrements of the trade can act as an antidote for the growing plague of boredom. Most dealers are proud of fine scales, and enjoy the ritual of sifting and weighing their stock. The exchange, sometimes involving large amounts of cash and drugs, is the climax of the business and may involve an 007 sort of intrigue.

Consider a situation where a dealer wants to buy three pounds of pot. He searches for a "connection" and eventually finds one, the proverbial "friend of a friend." At a pay

phone, he arranges to meet the connection at a corner on
the Lower East Side, and agrees on the price. He is there
at the specified time, meets the connection, and they go to
a nearby apartment. There, the dealer shows his money
and the connection brings out the grass, tightly pressed
into one-pound blocks and bound in heavy paper. The
dealer opens each block and "tastes" it, smoking a little to
judge the quality. Satisfied, he hands over the money,
packs the grass in a shopping bag, and heads for home to
split it up into smaller quantities and resell it.

A smaller deal, perhaps selling an ounce of pot, is much
simpler, a matter merely of acquaintance and cash. A
larger deal, in quantities of pounds or kilos, is a delicate
transaction demanding confidence, collateral, and coordination, especially to avoid the danger of being robbed or
"burned." In exchanges of ten pounds and up—a
hundred-kilo (220-pound) deal is not unheard of in the
East Village—a gun is often around.

A large deal involving kilos of marijuana has a singular
mystique for the dealer. Few hippie dealers are aware of
the route of the shipment from the field, or the size of the
original load of grass arriving in the city. The route behind their own connection is a shadowy one, laced with
rumors of organized crime and the Mafia. To many independent dealers, the Mafia represents the jaws of hell.
"The Mafia," said a new-breed dealer, "is the Antichrist in
the world of drugs." Yet, at the same time, most dealers
are convinced that their commodities at some point pass
through Mafia hands.

A considerable amount of bargaining skill is needed for
success in dealing large quantities of drugs. The prices of
marijuana, LSD, and the amphetamines (the staple drugs
in the East Village, although hashish, cocaine, DMT, and

mescaline are occasionally available) fluctuate considerably. The successful dealer is able to play the market, buying when prices are low and selling when drugs are in demand. The typical dealer lacks the capital for this, and his business is more tenuous. The original hope of quick wealth fades and the dealer must ride with the tidal drug market to realize any profit. "You get hung up with all the hassle," said one, "and it becomes a full-time preoccupation."

There is little technical skill needed in dealing marijuana. With pharmaceutical drugs, such as LSD and the amphetamines, the dealer should be able to measure dosages. Large quantities of LSD usually come in crystal form which must be dissolved into solution and meted out in doses. LSD is measured in micrograms, millionths of a gram, and incompetent chemistry, which is common, can be disastrous. Usually, however, an acid accident results in doses that lack potency, rather than massive overdoses, an aggravating blessing for the consumer.

The key to success in dealing is the connection, the wholesaler. The bigger the connection, the better the business. (The ideal connection is one who can supply any quantity of any drug at any time for a good price.) For the larger the quantity one deals, or the nearer the source, the larger the profit per transaction. The risk increases, in the eyes of the dealer, more significantly in the number of transactions than in the increase in quantity.

A good connection is hard to find, and a dealer guards his connection's identity as General Motors guards its research lab. For if his customers discover his connection, the dealer will no longer be needed as a middleman. There are even people who act as brokers or agents, merely arranging deals for a percentage of the profit or a commission. Their career depends on confidence.

It's a closed profession, and there is no attempt to enlighten the consumer. Few people who buy ounces of drugs are aware of the prices of pounds or kilos, nor are they aware of the profit involved.

Risk, of course, is the basis of the whole game. It's a dangerous profession, and the primary danger is getting caught or "busted." The first bust usually marks the end of the youthful dealer's career. In New York, at least, a twenty-year term is not likely. With a good attorney, a first conviction will probably get a suspended sentence, with instructions to seek psychiatric care and lead a clean life. Moreover, with more stringent safeguards against search and seizure, admissible evidence is hard to find and a conviction is far from automatic. In any case, after the first arrest, suspicion is cast and the essential anonymity is lost. The refugee from the middle class usually must then retire from the dealing game.

Dealers vary in the ways they regard the threat of getting busted. Some merchants, like some consumers, live in constant fear. "Paranoid" is a word heard often. Few dealers have never suspected that their phone was being tapped and, of course, few dealers sell drugs to strangers. Extreme cases, often people who have been arrested before, may live as recluses, having a few trusted assistants to whom they "front" drugs to sell for a commission. Yet the typical dealer, although cautious, is nonchalant, and well aware that the first arrest is not likely to lead to prison. "It reaches the point where it's not worth the hassle," said a nineteen-year-old marijuana merchant. "If I get busted, I get busted."

Another occupational hazard is the danger of getting "burned." The novice dealer is particularly prey to this. It is a simple operation, the connection demanding cash in advance, and going out to pick up the drugs. Of course, he doesn't return. The customer waits long past the time of the promised delivery, slowly realizing that he's been burned. It is a common practice on all levels of dealing. Only the consequences may vary. The teeny-bopper on MacDougal Street who buys a "nickel" ($5.00 worth) of marijuana and gets a nickel's (five cents') worth of oregano has little recourse. The East Side dealer who buys a thousand doses of worthless LSD can, and often does, try to correct the deal. He may start with threats; he may finish by hiring some "muscle" to break the offender's arm. On higher levels of dealing, but still among hippies, there can be physical danger. There are guns in the East Village, and there are vendettas.

Dealing, like gambling, is a hard profession to retire from. It becomes an involuntary commitment, combining debts, financial ambitions, and a fascination with the whole game. Some leave as a success. Some quit, and some go back to college. All acknowledge the fascination. "It's schizophrenic," said a Long Island youth. "On the one hand, you're an antidote to organized crime, and a mercenary because of the profit; on the other hand, you're a psychedelic Jehovah's Witness, looking for the millennium when drugs are legal." Legalization, most of the new-breed dealers agree, would be a fitting end to their profession.

AMPHETAMINE APPLE IN EDEN

Amphetamine is the apple of the Underground. It has a lot of bites in it, ominously indicating that today's Adam and Eve, now hippies, cannot be satisfied with the ecstasy of their psychedelic Eden. The amphetamine apple is a well-kept secret in the Underground, perhaps justified by the fear that, if the word got out, today's deities might start eviction proceedings.

In the last decade, amphetamine has been conveniently and quietly accepted by the American culture. It is a drug tailored to the temptations of the times. For the executive and for those striving to succeed him, for anyone overcome with delinquent demands, it is an elixir of energy, a solution to the deadline dilemma, an antidote to drudgery. It offers a seductive illusion of brilliance and an abundant supply of enthusiasm.

The use of amphetamine (here referring to a class of stimulant drugs including Benzedrine, Dexedrine, Methedrine, and compounds) within the Establishment is discreet. The physician is a peer. He may understand the pressures and appreciate the patronage. There is no need for the suburban amphetamine consumer to be concerned about Federal and State laws prohibiting its illicit use. He regards his own use as legitimate, notarized by his doctor's prescription. He would, in fact, probably approve of the laws, assuming that they exist to combat narcotics addiction and the burgeoning use of drugs by young people. He would regard as slanderous any suggestion that he had a great deal in common with "dope fiends." For the lifeblood of the suburban amphetamine scene is rationalization, the essence hypocrisy, the irony obvious.

Amphetamine, therefore, crosses party lines. The housewife who takes gradually increasing doses of amphetamine each morning to "wake up" is closer than she cares to believe to the A-head who concedes that he shoots the same drug to "get high." There are, of course, differences. In the suburbs, drug consumption is a private matter. In the Underground, amphetamine has led to a mutually reinforcing subsociety. It is ironic that the Underground, the prey of the Food and Drug Administration (FDA), probably has a better understanding of the drug than its suburban counterpart. Within a society united by a drug, its effects become rapidly apparent. The drug, be it amphetamine, heroin, or the psychedelic, is an inexhaustible topic for conversation. The eccentricities of the drugs and the experiences of the users constitute the folklore of the Underground. The novice is taught how to smoke a joint of marijuana, how to cope with psychedelic surprises, and how to survive on a steady diet of amphetamine. He soon learns how to recognize and exploit the effects of the drug, which is the secret of "getting high."

Based on an astonishingly accurate understanding of the drug's potential, the Underground takes amphetamine seriously. Amphetamine-heads are a distinct group, semi-quarantined, and often regarded with apprehension by fellow hippies in different scenes. The psychedelic scene especially recoils at amphetamine and, perhaps sensing the apple analogy, tries to ignore the blight in their Eden. Amphetamine, with its physically devastating consequences, may occupy the position heroin once did: the step too far. And, although its effects are the opposite of the depressant opiates, amphetamine habituation can be as engulfing as today's watered-down heroin addiction. The A-head, like the heroin addict, is susceptible to the dangers of a massive overdose or hepatitis from a used needle. Unlike the heroin addict, the A-head runs the risk of serious, and permanent, brain damage. "The amphetamines and barbiturates," said Dr. Marie Nyswander, a pioneer in battling heroin addiction, "are the worst drugs we have for brain damage."

At what point does the hippie bite the amphetamine apple? Usually amphetamine in earnest follows considerable experience with the psychedelic drugs and a preparatory period of bored stagnation in the Underground. As a stimulant, it can be a temporary antidote to boredom. As a habit, it replaces boredom. The amphetamine introduction is an energetic, enthusiastic, and seductive experience. As the novice progresses, he builds up tolerance to the drug, requiring larger doses to maintain the effect. Eventually he may discover the sensory excitement in the amphetamine inferno: the Niagara "rush" after injecting the drug, the wonder of being "spaced," the hell of the "come-down." To understand amphetamine, you have to think in terms of space.

You can force your body to function on an amphetamine diet for several days. Soon you will be "spaced" and well into the timeless oblivion of an amphetamine vigil. The stomach is tight and empty. It is an ideal fast, unencumbered by hunger. The nerves are taut, senses overtuned, mind and body glutted with impotent energy, but

you are high, spaced, and cluttered reality shimmers
around you. Being spaced is a pace of mind. The pace is
accelerated by the perpetual, haunting illusion that something is catching up behind you. For diversion, you can
strain the senses, dissolve into raga rock blasting through
earphones, lose yourself in the flashing energy of a strobe
light, and submerge in environmental madness. It doesn't
hurt. The body seems beyond pain, the senses beyond
protest.

The come-down is inevitable. The amphetamine come-
down is the vague, nebulous, sometimes terrifying and
always unpleasant state between the time the effects of
the stimulant wear off and the time you go to sleep or take
another dose. It may be a long, clumsy descent, pocked
with slumps of depression, disillusion, and disgust, and
laced with boredom and exhaustion. Or a come-down
may career, and all the amphetamine debris is intensified,
the depression unbearable. The intensity may vary, generally relative to the amount taken, but the come-down is
unpredictable. The apocalyptic come-down may come
without warning or preparation. Then begins the desperate, frenzied search for a parachute drug. One East Side
dealer is a "saint" to many A-heads, for he keeps an
emergency supply of barbiturates in case of particularly
vicious come-downs. As a last resort, there is cheap wine.
And finally sleep.

Being spaced and coming down are day and night to
the confirmed A-head. His occupation could be called
energy disposal. Amphetamine is a vigorous drug, a store-
house of unrelenting energy, and a mirage-maker of elu-
sive mind-scapes, of enthusiasms and good intentions.
When the only goal is to get high, the energy has no
direction. It doesn't wait to be called. The classic outlet is

talking—rapping—an endless, breathless monologue of trivia. The enthusiasms may be realized by composing long lists. Any activity will do, just for the sake of doing it, as an interim in the amphetamine ping-pong of obsession and distraction.

Amphetamine is not a psychedelic drug, like marijuana and LSD. The drugs seem to occupy opposite poles in the Underground, in almost a Blakean perspective of Heaven and Hell. Paradoxically, Underground folk medicine has found that the drugs may complement each other. Amphetamines and barbiturates may be used to navigate LSD trips more precisely. A small amount of amphetamine is sometimes taken beforehand to ensure a smooth take-off, or during the session to increase altitude. Barbituates can ground the flight in minutes. And marijuana is often used to soothe the amphetamine experience, to take off the rough edges, to invite introspection, to get more spaced.

The choice of drugs depends on the desired effect. If the sole aim is to get high or spaced, there is a wide selection. When a favorite drug is scarce, there are substitutes. Thus the junkie will sometimes take amphetamine, the A-head LSD, balancing ups with downs in the laboratory of his body.

On the other extreme is the person who seeks enlightenment instead of sensation. He may be an occasional user of psychedelic drugs, sometimes a confirmed acidhead. Amphetamine has no place in his metaphysical quest for illumination. An amphetamine come-down is not compatible with the love-joy-ecstasy trip. The ecstasy camp regards the A-head with apprehension. And, cautious of their own tenuous respectability, the psychedelic community has distracted attention away from the black sheep of the family.

Amphetamine is not physiologically addicting. Technically it is habituating, and rare is the comparable habit. The housewife conditioned to facing the morning with a stimulant would have a hard time without it. Once a student has discovered "bennies," he finds it impossible to cram all night with coffee. For the hippie conditioned to taking drugs, the amphetamine temptation is more than enough. The pattern is well established. Tolerance increases, dosage increases, dependence increases. Seeking a more powerful sensation, he usually evolves from taking it orally, to "snorting" it—sharply inhaling the powder into the nostrils—then, to injecting it. When he has reached the stage of injecting amphetamine at fairly regular intervals, he has joined the A-head community.

There is a certain camaraderie among A-heads, based partially on a variety of needs which incline the misery-loving company to stick together. First is supply. A-heads, like junkies, often retail their drug to support their own habits. Unlike marijuana and LSD, which are diffused throughout the Underground, the supply of methedrine is generally confined to devotees. And within the community are some who help a novice. At least by example, he may be taught how to survive: how to eat without hunger, how to rest without sleep. He may be taught how to shoot up, a highly delicate task, or a veteran will do it for him. He will learn how to assemble "works," the tube from an eyedropper, a nipple from a baby bottle, and where to find the precious needle. And a fellow A-head understands. He understands the rapping monologue and all other outlets of amphetamine energy to which an outsider might overreact. He understands the spaced-out oblivion and the cascading come-down because he's in it, too. And that means a lot.

Few A-heads live alone. If they have an apartment, they will soon have company. The A-head camaraderie is strong enough to have created fledgling communities, perhaps fifteen in a loft. An amphetamine apartment is a distinctive dwelling; clutter competes with examples of obsessed meticulousness. A carpet could be picked free of dust by hand while dishes fester in the sink. Evidence of amphetamine energy diffusion is everywhere: cryptic phrases scrawled on walls, constructions of mechanical refuse. The energy obviously becomes hard to direct. Weeks of stale garbage and moldy dishes combined with human amphetamine decay, a frenzied decay, can bring visions of *Marat/Sade*.

For, in spite of the social safeguards, decay sets in. The body is weakened by a sporadic, insufficient diet, a diet of demanded bulk, uninspired by appetite. The body is depleted of energy and, oblivious to the body's barren resources, another shot of amphetamine promises rejuvenation. The common cold is a major threat to A-heads.

While the body decays, the mind may grow numb from the amphetamine cycle. Countless come-downs show their effect. And if the novice is prey to the amphetamine illusions, the veteran is captive. The game of keeping track of reality becomes confusing, the confusion becomes boring, and some finally quit. They are the amphetamine mutants.

Most A-heads stabilize or pull out before they reach the mutant stage. Others, an undocumented few, succumb to a massive overdose, or hepatitis, or the impact of a virus on a vulnerable body. Ironically, most A-heads seem to be aware of the decay-destruction possibilities of the drug, but are not inhibited by the danger. Such is the amphetamine seduction.

Eden may be in for a come-down.

HUNCKE THE JUNKIE

My phone rang on a hot morning in July and it was Allen Ginsberg.

"Do you know Herbert Huncke?" Ginsberg asked. "Have you ever met Huncke?" I said that I hadn't.

"He's the oldest living junkie in New York," Ginsberg said, "and an old sidekick of Burroughs and Kerouac. He turned Burroughs on to junk and he's waiting in line at Manhattan General to get in so he can cut down on his habit. He's been waiting for four days and he thinks he can get in in about twenty minutes, and he needs his suitcase which is in his hotel room, so can you go up to the hospital and get his key, and go to the hotel and get his suitcase and take it to him? He's wearing a white sweater. Hurry!"

I threw on some clothes and rushed to the subway, and in maybe nineteen minutes was running down 21st Street to the back door of Manhattan General where the junkies wait in line to save their lives. Huncke met me in the middle of the block. His white cardigan sweater was unmistakable, but so was his face, which was fragile testimony to thirty years on heroin.

Huncke had decided to save Manhattan General for another day, but he insisted on showing me the junkies' lobby. The floor behind the door was strewn with cigarette butts, and the air was a dense fog. They leaned against the wall—men, women, white, Puerto Rican, black —and sat on the benches. All the openings, the sign-in windows and such, were caged. It was as hard to get in as it was to get out.

And then as we walked over to Ginsberg's, Huncke began to rap. Huncke raps beautifully, the sound of his magnificent voice—all that seems intact in his devastated body—as tantalizing as the content. He has so much to rap about, the days with Burroughs, the trials and woes of Ginsberg, the gilded gossip about the beats a decade ago and last week. It is all that he has, his memories and a talent for recalling them. It is not quite enough, but he gets by.

When we arrived, Ginsberg took me aside. "Whatever you do," he said sternly, "don't give him money! I'm not kidding. Be careful. He's very persuasive."

And then he took Huncke aside, and asked him to spare me the touch. "He's just a kid," he said, "and he doesn't have very much money." And then Huncke hit Ginsberg for ten bucks.

Huncke is a master of the touch. It's his livelihood, and as I walked with him back to the West Side I braced myself to follow Ginsberg's orders and resist the inevitable climax of the conversation. It never came. Huncke spared me—this first time—waved goodbye, and promised to stop by and visit.

And he did stop by, roughly once a week at a punctual

nine o'clock in the morning, at an old loft I had on Prince Street that summer. I would try to wake up and make some coffee and we would sit and talk for three hours or so, the same glorious rap, and then he would hit me for $5.00 or so, always, he said, for a hotel or some other non-narcotic necessity of life. And I would give it to him, because he had earned it.

Toward the end of the summer he passed a bad check on me and disappeared. I was sad that he never came back, and, in lieu of an autograph, pasted the check, which he had endorsed in various styles of script, on the title page of his *Journals*, a rambling collection of recollections that had been published by the Poet's Press. A little while later I heard that he was in jail.

After he had finished six months in jail, he drove to San Francisco with a friend. I suspected that he was intrigued by the talk about a "Love Community" in Haight-Ashbury and the Diggers' free money.

He liked the city, but was disappointed by the people, and a few weeks ago he was back in New York, but he didn't get much of a homecoming. Ginsberg was in Italy and Panna Grady, a long-time patron, was in London, and Peter Orlovsky was in a surly mood. He had spent the money Ginsberg had left to get him to London. And again, the line at Manhattan General proved to be too long for his patience. He stooped to selling salt pills as acid tabs. And all the people he supposedly burned were rumored to be waiting for his up-coming reading at St. Mark's-in-the-Bouwerie. It seemed that, for once, the audience would be taking the collection. But, deft as ever, Huncke survived the reading and went off to rap with Neal Cassady.

The other day he came by to visit again, and we sat in a

bar on Seventh Avenue and talked. Huncke had a coke—
he is repulsed by liquor—and I asked him to recall again
how he came to meet William Burroughs.

"I met Bill in 1944," he said. "I had just come back
from a trip to South America. Bill had met a friend of
mine from Cleveland, a guy like something from a Humphrey Bogart movie, with padded shoulders, a felt hat
and a flashy tie. He had a job as a soda jerk around
Columbia. I think his intention was to case the neighborhood. And Burroughs approached him and asked if he
could get rid of a sawed-off shotgun. Burroughs always
had a sort of interest in the underworld. So this friend
brought Burroughs down to my apartment, with the gun
and several gross of morphine Syrettes. When I first saw
Burroughs I thought he was a Treasury agent.

"He thought he'd like to try the morphine just once. We
turned him on. He was a natural. The next thing we knew
he joined forces with us."

Burroughs was then at Columbia where he had,
Huncke recalled, "a coterie which included Kerouac and
Allen, who idolized him, and myself. I was sort of intro-
duced as an oddity that should be observed.

"At this same time, the Kinsey report was taking shape.
I had met Dr. Kinsey in Times Square, and I introduced
him to Allen and others. We used to get together in the
Angler Bar, which was off 42nd Street. We'd sit there and
talk and eat and drink. Bill was interested in karate. One
of the most interesting things I ever witnessed was Bill
trying to give a knockout blow with three fingers to break
up a fight. He had gathered his coat around him ele-
gantly, with all the dignity and reserved demeanor he
had, and he was trying to reach over the heads in the
brawl to hit the guy."

In 1947, Huncke and Burroughs went to Texas. "It was a beautiful year," Huncke said. "Just Bill, myself, his wife, and young Bill was born in July. We lived in a little weatherbeaten cabin on the edge of the bayou, and we raised a crop of pot. We were going to try to raise oriental poppies in a hothouse.

"Bill had his pistols and did target practice. He used to stand out there and draw with his pistols strapped to his side and shoot at the barn. Then Neal Cassady and Allen drove down from San Francisco. Neal and Bill and I drove back to New York in a jeep with the pot, and Allen took the train.

"I didn't see too much of Burroughs after that. Then Bill went to Tangiers, and I just hung around, hooked all the time, using junk, junk, junk. I've been using junk for more than thirty years. I can't write without it. I can't live without it."

He can't live without it. Herbert Huncke, apostle of junk, immortalized in more than one Kerouac novel, eulogized in Ginsberg's ravings, godfather to *Naked Lunch*. As he fumbled for a match in the bar on Seventh Avenue, I could see that it was time for him to go again in search of that small bag that holds his bones together.

I gave him the money to buy it, and I hoped that he would find it.

A LIGHT ON A VERY BLEAK STREET

Anyone who has returned to his car to find the lock picked from the inside and the sterling silver Christ from the dashboard on its way to the nearest fence knows how cunning a junkie can be. Anyone who watches a junkie friend reach the end of his rope for the sixteenth time only to bounce up from the jaws of disintegration and start the cycle all over again must marvel at the resilience of the addict. The junkie is, at once, a tribute to the survival instincts and a testament to the self-destructive capacities of man. Which is why, perhaps, the traditional spoon-fed "custodial" treatment of drug addiction is so often doomed to failure.

Odyssey House is ten months old. In a ramshackle green house in the heart of East Harlem, fourteen veterans of a collective century of addiction are helping each other back to humanity. They're doing it on their own. Nothing was set up for them. The group, financed solely by private contributions, has not received any public funds. Nor are they prisoners. There are no bars on the windows. At any time, they can walk down to the corner and cop a bag of heroin. It's easy in East Harlem. But they don't. They are committed to the project only by their own determination.

The leader of the group is Tony Enriques. Enriques,

thirty-eight, is friendly, articulate, and tough. Ten months ago, he was undergoing detoxification at Metropolitan Hospital for the fourteenth time in his ten years of addiction. Enriques was one of seventeen thousand cases that had been through Metropolitan Hospital in six years. His maintenance at the hospital cost $52.00 a day in public funds.

Enriques's "Odyssey" began at Metropolitan Hospital. There he met Drs. A. Ronald Sorvino and Judianne Densen-Gerber, who saw promise in the addiction research project of Dr. Efren Ramirez, now Coordinator of Addiction Programs for New York City, in Puerto Rico. "In order for the addict to assume some responsibility," Enriques explained, "you have to relinquish some to him. This wasn't possible at the hospital." Enriques, the doctors, and seventeen fellow veterans of many detoxifications left the hospital en masse in October 1966.

They first went to Daytop Lodge, a narcotics rehabilitation community in Staten Island, where they stayed for six days. "They invited us to join them," Enriques recalled, "but we declined. We had fifty dollars cash among eighteen of us. We were offered a log cabin in Bridgewater, Connecticut, until we could find a permanent place, and we used the money to send eleven of the group up there. Six of us and a pregnant girl were left here." Dr. Densen-Gerber housed them in sleeping bags in her East End Avenue apartment until they found the house.

The building, a seven-room house at 304 East 109th Street, had been vacant for some time. "It was a wreck," Enriques said. "The kids had broken in. Winos were sleeping downstairs. The windows were broken, the plumbing and the furnace were out, and the roof leaked." Businessmen and neighbors donated materials, and, only weeks out of Metropolitan Hospital, they began to put it back together.

They immediately established a good working relationship with the neighborhood. A delegation went to introduce themselves to the Twenty-third Precinct police headquarters, gave them a list of Odyssey House members, and invited the cops over for coffee. Not only did the cops accept the invitation, but they donated a coffee urn to the House. On NBC's "Today" show, Sergeant Hart and Captain Gross of the Twenty-third called Odyssey House "an oasis in the desert."

In marked contrast to the reception of many narcotics rehabilitation centers, the neighborhood welcomed Odyssey House with relief. The House is immaculate, and a model for the block. A nearby Italian bakery has donated bread every day.

Odyssey House functions on a rigid schedule, although it avoids the almost military self-discipline of the Synanon and Daytop groups. It also differs from the other communities in its emphasis on professional psychiatric assistance and its goal of rapid reintegration into the community. "Synanon is almost a lifetime thing," Enriques explains. "They've just created another subculture. We take a person who is almost totally dependent on society and make him an independent, productive person."

The group is structured on a series of levels, beginning with the raw addict who, once accepted, goes through the "candidate in" or induction period. There are four levels of in-residence treatment, which may last from ten to fifteen months. As they go through different levels, they assume different responsibilities. In the first level, the person takes orders, and doesn't like it. In the second level, he takes orders, realizing the need for authority. In the third level, he begins to give orders. And in the fourth level, he gives orders to himself. During this time, Enriques explains, the person is "learning to live with himself." When a person has completed the fourth level, he is proposed for "candidate out" and re-entry into society. This is the weaning period, generally six months long, when the candidate continues to live in the house, but may participate in job training or education outside. Finally, there is a five-year follow-up program.

Of the original eighteen who began the program in October, fourteen remain today, six months later. Two, including Enriques, have reached the "candidate out" level, and one is proposed for the level. Of the four who dropped out, three are trying to get back in. Readmission is far from automatic. "In order for them to place any value on the program," Enriques explains, "they have to earn it." They are given a series of appointments to discuss readmission, and are judged by how many they keep. "It's hard," he says, "because an addict is a kind of person who wants what he wants when he wants it. They go out, but they can't block out the learning experience. They get hooked, but they can't escape the truth of the matter. The drug doesn't quite do it anymore."

The daily routine in Odyssey House is much like a family, group therapy. Each person is exposed to twenty to thirty hours of group therapy a week, sometimes with one of the three part-time psychiatrists, sometimes only with "peer groups" chosen by age or level. "I'm like a parent," Dr. Densen-Gerber said. "There are times for the parent to be there, and times for the parent not to be there."

The quarters are cramped in the small house. Upstairs, men are jammed into two rooms, sleeping in triple-deck bunks they built themselves. The three women in the group share a room behind the tiny living room on the first floor. In the basement are an office and a kitchen. There is little privacy, and this is intentional. No secrets are tolerated. Nothing is considered too personal to be discussed. "You can be questioned on any aspect of your life," Enriques said. "It's up to each individual to challenge others and get them to move."

Household duties are considered very important. Lack of structure is a major problem in addiction. Each morning at 8:30, a house meeting is held to discuss the day's events and to consider any negligence. "We are constantly aware of small, detailed things that have led us to addiction," Enriques said. "We're not afraid to tell people. We have a saying, that if three people tell you you're a horse, you should put on a saddle."

Every day, the New York City Medical Examiner's Office performs urinalysis checks to confirm that the residents remain drug free. The members gladly consent. "We don't need it," Enriques said. "We know who's staying off. We haven't had one drug incident since we've been here."

The fourteen members of Odyssey House come from widely varied backgrounds, but, one explained, "the emotional ties here are almost the same as in a family." They are white, Negro, and Puerto Rican. Some attended college, some never reached high school. They range in age from nineteen to forty. Their addiction ranges from two to twenty-three years. They have had twenty-five children. They computed that in one year they had used $400,000 for drugs, or at least $1.2 million in stolen property, or roughly $90,000 apiece.

And yet, in less than a year in the therapeutic community, Odyssey House members are going out to help others conquer addiction. "You can't just work at treatment and ignore prevention," Enriques said. "We went to the civic groups, and invited them to come to the house. We've been to NYU, CCNY, Queensborough College, and many high schools. We're trying to make the public realize their responsibility in the problem of addiction. They should consider the consequences before opposing a rehabilitation center in their neighborhood. And they should employ rehabilitated addicts. What's the sense of being rehabilitated if you can't use anything you learn?"

Odyssey House is now incorporated as a nonprofit organization, and is a recognized rehabilitation center up to the Federal level. Soon, they will move from their cramped headquarters in East Harlem. A building has been found that will house sixty persons for long-term residence treatment. "We don't want to reveal the site yet," Enriques said. "Once we're there, we feel that the community will see that we're an asset, that we can be productive. We have something to offer. Being an ex-addict, I know what can work."

LOBBYING FOR TENDERNESS

Allen Ginsberg, lobbying for tenderness, bared a large part of his soul before a Senate sub-committee investigating the use of LSD.

"I'm here to tell you about my personal experiences," he began softly, "and am worried that without sufficient understanding and sympathy for personal experience, laws will be passed that are so rigid that they will cause more harm than the new LSD that they try to regulate."

The atmosphere was neither hostile nor sympathetic; rather, curiosity dominated as Ginsberg took the stand. He bowed, a small Buddhist bow, and tried to dispel some of the apprehension among the senators, press, and spectators in the floodlit, marbled caucus room. "Whatever prejudgment you have about me, or my bearded image, I hope you will suspend it so that we can talk together as fellow beings in the same room of Now, trying to come to some harmony and peacefulness between us."

His efforts were first to establish a common bond with those listening. He noted the common frustration with the lack of a place for the human, personal, individual factor in our society. It is "a feeling of being caught in a bureaucratic machine which is not built to serve some of our deepest feelings . . . a machine which closes down our senses, reduces our language and thoughts to uniformity, reduces our sources of inspiration and fact to fewer channels—as TV does—and monopolizes our attention with secondhand imagery—packaged news, as we're having it packaged now"—and the network cameras whirred softly—"and doesn't really satisfy our deeper needs—healthy personal adventure in an environment where we are having living contact with each other in the flesh, the human universe we are built to enjoy and live in.

"All this is inevitable," he said, "especially since we have come to value material extensions of ourselves." But he still emphasized the need for some respite. "Human contact is built into our nature as a material need as strong as food. . . . We can't treat each other only as objects—we can't treat each other as Things lacking sympathy. Our humanity would atrophy, be crippled, and die —*want* to die. Because life without feeling is just one more 'Thing,' an inhuman universe."

Ginsberg described experiences he had had using various psychedelic drugs. The purpose of the description was twofold. First, he further attempted to establish a rapport by sharing deeply personal experiences. He repeatedly expressed his fears that his candor would be rejected. Second, he "wanted to explain why that very personal thing has a place here," that these human experiences might be a possible refuge for a Person in this plastic world.

He spoke first of his early experiences with peyote, experiences which he has described in his poem "Howl" (a copy of which he submitted to the committee). The peyote vision "felt so strange and yet familiar, as if from another lifetime . . . like the myths of all religions, like the graceful appearance of a Divine Presence, as if a God suddenly made himself felt in my old weekly New York Universe." He spoke of his experiences with the psychedelic vine ayahuasca in Peru, and recounted his conversations with holy men in India. And he told of how a few nights before the Vietnam Day March in Berkeley last fall he, the novelist Ken Kesey and his Merry Pranksters, and the Hell's Angels "all had a party at the Hell's Angels' house."

Prior to this, Ginsberg said, "The public image of a violent clash between students and the Hell's Angels escalated in everybody's mind—like a hallucination." At the party, organized by Kesey, "most everybody took some LSD, and we settled down to discussing the situation and listening to Joan Baez on the phonograph, and chanting Buddhist prayers. We were all awed by the communication possible—everybody able to drop their habitual Image for the night and feel more community than conflict. And the evening ended with the understanding that nobody really wanted violence; and there was none on the day of the march."

Finally Ginsberg told of an LSD experience at Big Sur in the fall of 1965. It was his first in several years, he said, and was shortly before the Berkeley Vietnam demonstrations. "We were all confused . . . many angry marchers blamed the President for the situation we were in. I did, too. The day I took LSD was the same day that President Johnson went into the operating room for his gall bladder illness. As I walked through the forest wondering what my feelings toward him were . . . the awesome place I was in impressed me, with its old trees and ocean cliff's majesty. Many tiny, jeweled, violet flowers along the path of a living brook that looked like Blake's illustration for a canal in grassy Eden: huge Pacific water shore. I saw a friend dancing, long-haired, before giant green waves, under cliffs of titanic nature that Wordsworth described in his poetry, and a great yellow sun veiled with mist hanging over the planet's ocean horizon. Armies at war on the other side of the planet . . . and the President in the valley of the shadow—himself experiencing what fear or grief? I realized that more vile words from me would send out negative vibrations into the atmosphere—more hatred against his poor flesh and soul on trial—so I knelt on the sand, surrounded by masses of green kelp washed up by a storm, and prayed for President Johnson's tranquil health."

Ginsberg had tried to dispel the apprehension about the psychedelic experience as gently as he had done with the apprehension about himself. It was a formidable task. The hearings to date had had the cold aura of a scientist examining something wriggling under his microscope, a germ, perhaps, a "menace," in the words of Chairman Thomas Dodd. He didn't like the looks of it, but was determined to find out what it was. Ginsberg, to use liberal analogy, was archy the cockroach come to life, telling depression-ridden America of the 1930's to be gentle and look at themselves. But America still stomped on roaches and Ginsberg's testimony may have been equally futile against the "Just the facts, ma'am" scrutiny of the Sub-Committee on Juvenile Delinquency. He was not rebuked. More likely, he received the much-taunted "white liberal" treatment. He was smiled at and ignored.

He had pointed out the need for a self-liberating experience, a need which everyone, consciously or not, shares, and he gave examples of personal experiences with psychedelic drugs which, for him, had helped to fulfill this need. Ginsberg now went on "to offer some data to calm the anxiety that LSD is some awful mind-bending monster threat which must be kept under lock and key."

Ginsberg offered three main ideas regarding this anxiety. He suggested that "there has been a journalistic panic exaggeration of the LSD danger," noting as an example wide discrepancies in the news reports on a young Brooklyn girl who had accidentally swallowed a cube of LSD. He provided statistics showing that "there is negligible danger to healthy people in trying LSD and comparatively little danger to most mentally sick people," and he urged the committee not to disregard "the appearance of religious or transcendental or serious, blissful experience through psychedelics" and suggested that they "treat LSD with proper humanity and respect."

When he had finished his statement, Ginsberg was questioned by Senators Jacob Javits of New York and Quentin Burdick of North Dakota, who was Acting Chairman in Dodd's absence. Many of the questions seemed to be the standard ones asked of the "pro-LSD" witnesses in these hearings, for instance, on the source of the drugs. One could not help but get the impression that such questions were asked merely to get them on the record. When asked where he obtained the drugs, Ginsberg replied that "in order to speak freely on the subject, I've had to stop my use. I have heard that the Narcotics Bureau has been trying to set me up for an arrest." Burdick prodded: "You don't know where it comes from?" "I literally do not know," he replied. At this point, Javits reminded Ginsberg of his privilege against self-incrimination. Other witnesses, when asked about the source, almost invariably said that they had obtained the drugs from "friends." The consistency of the "friends" answer became almost a joke to the committee, evoking some laughter.

Although Javits had spoken amiably with Ginsberg a number of times before his testimony, his questioning became somewhat sharp, though far short of the harsh Teddy Kennedy–Timothy Leary exchange in the same room a few weeks before. Javits repeatedly reminded Ginsberg that he was not qualified to testify on any of the medical aspects of LSD. "Do you consider yourself qualified to give medical advice to my sixteen-and-a-half-year-old son?" Javits asked. Javits indicated that he was concerned about Ginsberg's influence "among young people" and wanted to make it clear that the poet should not give "medical advice."

As he concluded his statement, Ginsberg suggested that "if we want to discourage use of LSD for altering our attitudes, we'll have to encourage such changes in our society that nobody will need to take it to break through to common sympathy." He suggested that the new generation, many of whom have experienced this "new sense of openness" will "push for an environment that is less rigid and mechanical, less dominated by automatic cold-war habits. A new kind of light has broken through upon our society—despite all the anxiety it has caused. Maybe these hearings are a manifestation of that slightly changed awareness. I wouldn't have thought it possible to speak like this a year ago. That we're more open to each other is the new consciousness itself: to reveal one's visions to a congressional committee!"

IS ACID OBSOLETE?

During a brief cease-fire recently, acid pro Dr. Richard Alpert came to chat with the administrator of the Los Angeles office of the Bureau of Drug Abuse Control. The administrator was coolly cordial; Alpert was beaming.

"You'll be happy to know that we've solved the LSD problem," Alpert began.

"How?" The administrator was suspicious.

"STP," said Alpert.

"What's that?" asked the administrator.

Alpert began talking about fuel-oil additives, and the administrator smiled weakly. Alpert was reassuring. "Don't worry," he said. "They have quality control in the labs."

If the LSD problem hasn't quite been solved, it may seem minor in the months to come. STP is a new psychedelic drug which, since its arrival in New York, has become the most sought-after high on the psychedelic scene. Free samples have been carefully distributed to experienced acid-heads, and perhaps one hundred New Yorkers have taken the STP trip. A number of "bad trips" have been reported, even among LSD veterans. But survivors are enthusiastic. On the basis of their reports, LSD may be obsolete.

Not only is the drug stronger and longer than LSD, it is reputed to have a permanent, cumulative effect, leading an early STP expert to call the drug "a specific mutant agent." Moreover, it seems to be a carefully planned circumvention of drug control. Unlike LSD and the major psychedelic drugs to date, STP has no pharmacological history. No patents have been filed. No chemical abstracts have appeared. It is rumored that a substance has been added to the little white pills which will obscure the chemical composition in the event of a spectrum analysis. The ingredients, needless to say, are a precious secret.

The most recurrent message about STP is a warning. The drug is new, powerful, and unpredictable. Unlike LSD, there are no "maps" for the trip and no experienced "guides." The errant explorer is strictly on his own. The medical aspects of STP are still a complete mystery. The potential for disaster is obvious.

Alpert discussed STP before a recent meeting of the Jade Companions, a hippie "protective association," at the Second Avenue headquarters of the Millennium Film Workshop. His comments were brief, but they added some substance to the deluge of rumors on the East Side about the drug.

All veterans concur on the overwhelming power of STP. They speak of a maelstrom of relentless energy. "A feeling," said Alpert, "that it's going to do it to you whether you like it or not." The energy seems to manifest itself physically. "You feel like your body is a conductor for tens of thousands of volts," said a user. "I was desperate for a ground." People tripping on STP physically tremble with the energy sensation. It is a stretching, quivering, shaking experience. Many have emerged from STP with a sudden concern for physical health. "We have to be strong," said one. "We need protein. The macrobiotic diet is bad news."

The relentless rush of energy is often a frightening experience. "Acid is like being let out of a cage," explained one user. "STP is like being shot out of a gun. There's no slowing down or backing up. You feel like your brakes have given out."

"At least for me," Alpert said, "there was a way to hide with LSD. I didn't get that with STP.

"In the middle of it," he continued, "I was screaming for Timothy [Leary]. TIM! Come help me! When Timothy was taking it for the first time, he called for Richard. It scares you."

A key to survival in the STP experience seems to be an ability to surrender to the energy flow of the drug. Resisting the rush or holding back can lead, many report, to an incredibly frustrating, up-tight experience.

STP seems to lack the disorientation of acid. Although the audio and visual hallucinations are vivid, a girl explained, "everything looks like it does when you're straight. It's like being on the other side of a glass wall. There also seems to be less identity confusion than under LSD. You know who you are," she said. Many have found that they could easily function—make telephone calls, find cabs—shortly after the peak of the STP experience. These things can be difficult to do after an intense LSD experience.

Another recurring report about STP is a sensation of timelessness. Alpert calls it "a totally NOW orientation." Past and future seem to dissolve in an electric present. "As time was lost," Alpert recalled, "I felt that I had lost something human. I felt that I had lost my humanity."

But the most enticing, and clearly the most disturbing, aspect of STP is that, unlike LSD, it seems to have a cumulative effect. It is a long trip to begin with. The direct effects last about fourteen hours, and a stoned aftermath may continue until sleep.

The next morning, many STP initiates have discovered that they still felt high, or at least "different." It is a mild feeling, but a persistent one. Generally rated a "good" feeling, it seems to last indefinitely.

"It's reasonable to ask what the hell is going on," said Alpert. "Are these the same things we were saying about LSD?"

"There is a mystique growing up around it," Timothy Leary commented. "It exposes your personal game to microscopic analysis. People seem to come out of it much straighter about themselves."

Some people claim to have discovered intense telepathic powers in STP. Another curious aspect of STP, a user explained, is that at the peak of the experience you tend to think that everyone else has taken the drug. He described his experience:

"I got out of the cab on St. Mark's Place. It was three in the morning and the street was full of people, standing around. The sky was glowing, like it was flaming. I thought it was the Second Coming or something. I was absolutely convinced that It had just happened, or would happen in seconds. And I thought everyone else knew it. How do you react when you're convinced? I was completely out of control."

The scant history of the drug only intensifies the mystery. The name STP (rumored to have been suggested by the Hell's Angels) was a playful attempt at confusion (another STP is a much-publicized motor oil ingredient). The catch is that the initials are the only identification of the drug. Without patents or chemical abstracts, it technically does not exist. The big question is whether the rumored additive can successfully obscure the secret ingredients.

"I don't know what's in it," Alpert told the meeting. "I don't want to know," he said darkly, "because somebody else will want to know soon."

The FDA is already tracking it down. A spokesman for the New York office of the Bureau of Drug Abuse Control was optimistic. "We have an idea of what it is," he said. "It may be just another name for LSD. If any is seized, it will naturally be analyzed. Then we'll know the exact chemical composition."

But until it is identified, it seems that STP will be legal. Identification is a prerequisite for control. If the additive can successfully obscure the chemical makeup of STP, the hands of the FDA might be tied.

THE SWAMI MAKES THE PEOPLE GLOW

Swami Satchidananda had been in Ceylon for five months, and the Integral Yoga Institute had lost some of the momentum that was so strong before when the Swami had been in New York. His people in New York are good friends, so they had not lost touch over his absence, but they were anxious to get back to work on the Hatha Yoga, and most anxious to see and dig their wonderful Swami.

His plane was due in from Paris at four in the afternoon. So around two his people gathered outside the Institute on West End Avenue to begin a caravan to JFK Airport. It was a beautiful spring afternoon and Swami's people were happy and smiling and hugging each other.

They piled in cars and drove to the airport and reassembled in the upper lobby of the International Terminal, where they waited for Swami's plane. They looked great, with bells and flaming colors and flowers. And they stood around the top of the escalators waiting and not talking very much and admiring the building.

One of them had a movie camera. He wound it and started to shoot. He was down on his knees and zooming in. Not much action. Just people waiting.

But suddenly there was an audience. The camera convinced a hundred other passengers that there was indeed something strange about the people in colors, just waiting around. They were making a movie. A hundred people formed a semicircle around Swami's people, watching them waiting, careful not to walk through the middle.

Swami's plane was late, and this went on for three hours.

But finally he arrived, and came through customs, beaming and radiant, and his people came to him loving, with garlands of flowers, and gathered around him to walk slowly a foot off the ground through the terminal, softly singing "Hare Om," into a Swami orange sunset behind the limousine outside.

Swami Satchidananda first came to New York a year ago in August. Conrad Rooks, a young millionaire who recalls his years as a junkie—and his escape from drugs—in a monumental personal epic film called *Chappaqua*, had met the Swami in his small ashram in Ceylon, where the Swami, a student of the great Swami Shivananda, had come in 1953 from the foothills of the Himalayas. Rooks was awed by the holy man. He sat with him and learned from him and paid his fare to travel around the world. When he was in Paris, the Swami met Peter Max, the New York artist, who urged him to come to the United States. He returned to New York with Max, intending only to stay two days.

But many people came to meet him, and he decided to stay longer. He started a few yoga classes in a suite at the Oliver Cromwell Hotel, and in the fall he opened the Integral Yoga Institute in a large apartment at 500 West End Avenue. The Institute was a success as his reputation spread, and in November his beaming countenance covered the town on posters which read: "ON DECEMBER 1, 1000 PEOPLE WILL BE ABLE TO HEAR SWAMI SATCHIDA-

NANDA." On December 11, Allen Ginsberg introduced the Swami to one thousand people, some of whom became his disciples. Swami Satchidananda has an ecstatic charisma that is hard to resist.

He looks like a Swami, with a great flowing mane of curling black hair that falls over his shoulders and out like a frame around his full silver beard. He wears saffron robes and his voice is deep and gentle and his smile is like a blessing. "He is so beautiful," said one of his students, "that he can get young people to fall in love with him and live under his guidance." But the man is inseparable from his message, which is yoga. It may begin with classes in asanas, or yoga postures, at the Institute. "You do asanas for a week and you can feel it," a student said. "Maybe you can feel peace for a few minutes by closing your eyes and listening to your heart beat."

The tangible results of yoga appeal to many youths who have experimented with psychedelic drugs. "Kids have been spoiled by acid," a student said. "They won't accept anything unless they can feel it." Many of the students at the Institute are psychedelic veterans, and they are slowly weaning themselves off drugs in a gentle transition from an artificial high to a natural one. Many feel that psychedelic drugs were an important preparation for yoga but, one smiled, "on drugs, you come down."

The Swami does not approve of the psychedelics, but he is patient with his students. "I never ask them to stop," he said. "I never force them.

"These drugs are powerful and hypnotic," he said. "The conscious mind is enslaved. If a person allows himself to be hypnotized very often, he becomes a subject. He loses his strong will. Certain dormant psychic forces are rushed up, and so suddenly that the body is shattered. If a person is weak, it is like running an old car on aviation petrol. And how can a chemical give you certain knowledge?

"They say that they want to expand their consciousness," he said. "That means that they are already yoga-conscious. The drugs fail them, so they come here."

The evolution from drugs is only part of the change among Swami's people. Some have given up meat, to follow a yogic vegetarian diet. Others have learned enough yoga in less than a year to begin to teach classes themselves. All give testimonials to the power of yoga.

"I've seen myself and many of my friends change," one said. "It wasn't easy. I had to vomit up a lot of conditioning to be able to chant 'Om.' But I've stopped being the skeptic that I was. I've stopped the constant analysis. I've become a much more peaceful person."

They have recently developed into a cohesive group that might be called a tribe, and they are now at the stage where they are considering the prospect of communal living. An important step in this evolution was the Electric Lotus, a tribal store which the Swami's people opened recently on East 6th Street. Although the store isn't directly affiliated with the Institute, the profits help to support the group and may someday support a community or ashram. It also serves as a focal point for the group on the East Side, and was a test to see if the group could work and function together.

Since the Swami returned from Ceylon in May, the group has progressed with astonishing speed. Other tribes may come to follow their model. A teacher is a great advantage. They are aware of it, and they revere the Swami. "He is a living ideal and a focal point for us as a group," one said. "His wisdom not only emanates from him now, but from all of us."

The Swami is also aware of the evolution, and of the youth movement of which it is a part. "I feel that there is some higher force that is taking care of these youths," he said, "and I think it's that force that brought me here.

"America has everything, and it should have yoga too."

GARY SNYDER, DOUBTER OF CITIES

"My two heroes, so to speak, are Chief Joseph on the one hand, the Nez Perce chief, and the Dalai Lama on the other." It was Gary Snyder talking. It couldn't have been anyone else.

Snyder had come to New York to read his poetry at the Guggenheim, to arrange for the publication of his latest book, *The Back Country*, and to march in a peace parade to Times Square. He was uncomfortable in the metropolis. "The thing is, I don't believe in cities. I think New York should be leveled and made into a buffalo pasture."

A veteran of Pacific Northwest lumber camps, Zen monasteries in Japan, and the San Francisco Underground, the poet reflects his experiences in his work. He prefaced a selection of new poems at the Guggenheim reading with the warning that "they may sound different than your expectations." They did. The new poems were a radical departure from the warm, mellow word-sounds of his earlier work. "Something is happening here that I don't quite understand," the poet said of his work. "I'm just letting it happen. It's kind of obscure." Perhaps a clue may be found in his experiences.

To find out, I went to interview Snyder the next morning in the apartment of his friend Allen Ginsberg. Ginsberg was asleep. Snyder sipped tea out of a tin bowl as we spoke in the next room.

Snyder is thirty-six and has blond hair and beard and a ruddy complexion, probably due to years outdoors. A few weeks ago he was in Kyoto, Japan, where he had lived, with a few interruptions, for the past six years. He went to Japan to study Zen Buddhism. Now he is working on a Bollingen Foundation grant to study Zen monastery life and training methods. I asked him how Americans adapt to living in the monasteries.

"It's not just the Americans," he said. "There are Australians, Austrians, one Israeli man who comes and goes. All sorts. Ten years ago when I first went there the Japanese monks were very spooked by foreigners. But the opposite attitude has emerged because it turns out that foreigners know quite a bit about Buddhism and are very earnest in their application."

The monk's life is a rigorous one, Snyder explained. "It's an enormous stumbling block to Japanese as well as to Americans. There's no heat in the winter, and it can be very, very cold. The etiquette, manners, and rigors. Also the food, and the short hours of sleep. Even the Japanese have a lot of trouble with this. That's one of the reasons there aren't more Zen monks, because the Zen monk's life is a killing life. It breaks the health of a certain percentage of people."

Snyder is a lay person, not a monk, although he participates in the activities of his local monastery in the morn-

ing and evening, and lives there during intensive meditation weeks. He has a small Japanese house in Kyoto, near
the edge of town. I asked if he climbed in the mountains
as he often did in Washington and Oregon.

"Not what I'd call climbing, but a lot of hiking. Right
near my house is where the woods and the mountains
start, so I can walk off for days in the brush and walk into
little villages in the high parts where they grow rice on
terraces."

Peter Orlovsky walked in with the groceries. The phone
rang. Ginsberg stirred and Snyder answered it.

Snyder spoke for a few minutes and then brought the
phone to the kitchen table to get at least half of the
conversation down on tape. "Well, it's already here," he
said into the phone, "without anybody really having made
it happen, and we're going to try to carry it out into the
mountains and have branches in the city too. We've got
places in the mountains south of San Francisco where we
live without clothes, and some kids are experimenting
with making acorn mush. It's pretty funny. Well, Rexroth
has always said that something like this was bound to
happen, and everybody is delighted about it simply because it's so much fun. . . .

"I think there's a real revolution going on," he said after
hanging up the phone. "Somewhere below or outside the
level of formal politics. That's what Rexroth said several
years ago. He said the real battle today is between the
hips and the squares. If you really want to know what's
happening today, listen to Bob Dylan."

"How does Dylan articulate it?" I asked.

"I think he knocks around a lot, gets high, and then he
thinks about it and writes it down. That's how I think he
articulates it."

Snyder explained that he planned to come back to California in several years, after another trip to India and Southeast Asia, and work with friends "building a Western Buddhism and a community of Western Buddhism. We've followed the Japanese model blindly. For one thing, women and children are all around, you know, and the Japanese model is based on a culture where women don't participate very much. We have to make a way of life which is a women's, children's, lovers' Buddhism too. And also more goofy because Americans are more goofy and everyone smokes grass and everyone uses acid. We have to handle that smoothly and make it useful too. I think LSD has good potentialities which can be geared into Zen. Zen is for providing that calm, common-sense, orderly, daily life core, and daily life discipline. And also a basic sense of kindliness and compassion to bring back all the wilder trips and make them something you can use for people.

"At this point, I do believe it's worthwhile to try communities. I think that the communities that were tried in the past were tried prematurely when there was too much Western culture and Christianity hanging on people. But we're much freer now. God is dead and Western culture is on the way out. What's happening now, among other things, is the emergence of the vibrations, the music, the rhythms of all these nonwhite traditional cultures. Like in this country the American Indian is really coming back in a funny way. Like peyote and LSD are really the American Indian's revenge, because when they take peyote and LSD, especially out West, it flips them out completely toward nature. It makes them feel at home in nature in a funny way.

"Even the kids in Kansas who would have said, ten

years ago, 'Jesus, what a drag to be in Kansas. I want to get to New York.' I'm talking about the really hip people. They're all turned on to the differences between long-grass prairie and short-grass prairie, and how much they would dig living in a sod hut out on the plains. They're at home where they are, in other words. They're not looking for a place to go."

It was eleven o'clock. Snyder had to see his publisher and he, Orlovsky, and I climbed into the front seat of the family Volkswagen bus. Peter Orlovsky fought the traffic toward Sixth Avenue. Snyder viewed the traffic with obvious distaste.

"This is not very scientific," he continued, "but if we live on this continent long enough—we're beginning to have been here long enough—the ghosts of the actions and lives of the previous people will begin to sink into us. So it's not possible to say America has a short history. You see, my history includes the fifty thousand years of the American Indians. I feel that kind of depth. I feel it, I really do feel it, and I feel that every landscape has its own demands, its own styles, its own mythologies and colors which, curiously enough, one discovers very clearly. You discover it in a sense when one takes peyote or even acid, and you say, why, of course, that's why Mayan art looks that way, or that's why sandpaintings are the way they are.

"Also, you're putting yourself in touch with the old ecology. For example, you know Zen macrobiotic food theory. Part of it is that you should eat food that belongs to your region. So everybody's eating brown rice. Strictly speaking, they shouldn't do that. In this country, everybody should eat maize. You should make maize your staple, or you should make acorn flour your staple. The wealth of acorns in California was what made it possible for California to have one of the largest Indian populations in the nation."

Orlovsky pulled up in front of New Directions. The hero of Kerouac's *Dharma Bums* climbed out, waved, and was gone. Charles Reznikoff was right when he introduced Snyder at the Guggenheim. He said of the poet: "He doesn't fake anything. He has been there, and he takes us with him."

TRIBES AND TRIBULATIONS

THE GROUP IMAGE

I was feeling down Thursday night—one of those downs when even spending money seemed futile, and getting high would only make it worse. One of those downs which comes after missing three appointments with an editor when you need the bread to stay alive. And I had hung around the office until eight at night only to be denied a fourth chance. So I walked across town, lazy loping, in hope of some respite on the East Side.

The Stones had just been convicted, fucking setup harassment, and the Who called them scapegoats and the Monkees said it was "trajic." There was to be a demonstration tomorrow in front of the British Consulate, which could be a beautiful goof or, alternately, a drag. Roger Ricco stood in the black-light window on St. Mark's Place and we bitched about the heat, groaned about the Stones, and slowly, inevitably, the Group Image ambled up. . . .

The Group Image may be the reincarnation of the Manhattan Indians. It is as if they came back after three centuries, looked around, grumbled "You did everything but sink it," and set to work getting the ecology straight

again. They have an intuitive feeling for New York, as the
Grateful Dead have for Haight-Ashbury, as the Hopi have
for Taos. Somehow they thrive amid the soot of Second
Avenue. Somehow they emerge intact from wheeling and
dealing and hustling in the Establishment fortresses. The
premium energy of New York is somehow combustible—
with or without additives—in the Group Image engine.

Long ago in April, the Group Image presided over the
last rites of the Balloon Farm on St. Mark's Place. The
upstairs of the Dom, a large auditorium which had
evolved from Polish weddings to Warhol "Inevitables" to
a pseudo-community center for the East Side, had
reached the final stage of metamorphosis. It was sold to
become "The Electric Circus." The neighborhood purists
recoiled and, with intentions like Joshua at Jericho, joined
the Group Image the night before the end for a final tribal
fling.

The audience wandered in by accident or invitation.
There was no publicity and the show was free. Some of
the Group Image began the music on stage. Soon most of
the Group Image was on the stage—there are at least
thirty—and then the audience began to come up. The
stage was a tangled mass of bodies and the dance floor
was practically empty.

Then the Group Image, audience and all, seemed to
slide off the stage and onto the floor, and the stage was
barren. You couldn't tell the Group Image from the audience. The music just emerged from the middle of a freaking crowd. Hippies danced around the hall with tambourines and flutes. They banged bottles on the tables and
stomped their feet in time with the throbbing sound. The
Balloon Farm reeled with the rhythm, and the stage was
empty.

"We wanted to destroy the stage," one of the Group Image said. They did. As soon as everyone moved to the floor, the stage was dead and the Balloon Farm buried.

The Group Image defies labels. It's a tribe. It's a multimedia orchestra. It's an open-ended group with a penchant for anonymity that falls roughly between USCO and the Family Dog. "We're living Marshall McLuhan," a member explained. A nucleus of about twenty hard-core members contribute for the rent for a loft on Second Avenue, which serves as an energy center for Group Image projects ranging from posters to light shows to mass humming sessions. When two or more gather together and start to hum, they will probably be joined by twenty. The hum rises to a crescendo. The ceiling quivers and an enraged Chinese waiter runs up from the restaurant downstairs.

Sound unites the Group Image. Although only a few are experienced musicians, the tambourines, bells, and foot-stomping of the whole family are essential to the sound. "Music is a tool toward a new way of life," one said.

They break most of the rules of the music game. "We don't warm up. We don't tune up. We don't do anything like that. It's just sort of a mass sound that starts to happen." They don't play in sets. When the music stops, the dance is over. A core musician plays until he gets tired and another takes his place.

Their ambition is to destroy stages everywhere and turn people onto themselves. They want to bring audience involvement to the final phase where the distinction between entertainment and audience dissolves, where the audience, in fact, entertains itself.

"We don't want the audience to get into our thing; we

want to help them get to their own thing. We're a catalyst."

They have demonstrated this in six appearances on the
East Side. Group Image audiences are bound to freak.
After about an hour into the music, everything seems to
pass a threshold. The dancing gets wilder as people
groove on the energy. The Group Image sounds, amplified like thunder, crest and fall and crest again. People
dance who have never danced before. Some dance franti-
cally by themselves. Others lock arms in whirling circles.
They whoop like Indians. They fall writhing in pigpiles to
the floor. And the music never, never pauses.

"We're trying to put the music through the people, into
them," explained a member. "The audience has to go
through a learning process, to find out that they can roll
around on the floor without going through the cliché
movements."

It may seem strange in New York but it would be
nothing new to an anthropologist. The relentless rhythm
is hypnotic. Technology has added amplified guitars and
strobe lights, but the same things have happened for eras
in primitive rituals and Indian pow-wows. "We've done
nothing but start it all up again," a member said. Which is
all the more reason to call the Group Image a tribe.

The trend toward tribes has been going on in the
psychedelic movement for some time. New York's USCO,
a community with a visual arts–religious orientation, startled the art world two years ago with communal paintings
and pious anonymity. San Francisco's Diggers, the lepre-
chauns of Haight-Ashbury, feed and house the transient
hippie. Small tribes abound in San Francisco and are
beginning to appear in New York. They will undoubtedly
multiply.

What brings people together in a tribe? "You can't lose your personal thing," a girl explained. "You can only gain. The more energy you give, the more you get." There's a feeling of "oneness" in the Group Image. They came together by accident or intuition. They are artists, dancers, musicians, high school dropouts, college graduates, a few kids, a few dogs, and a cab driver. "We need more women, though," one complained.

The tribe usually gathers at their loft in the late evening. The Group Image is open to any obsessions and their projects are myriad. Silk-screened campaign posters —the Abolafia for President campaign, the Plant Your Seeds campaign—are spread out drying, while an assembly line turns out more. A case of bubble gum, an anonymous gift, lies open on a drafting table. A sign on the wall reads: "COME TO CHARLIE'S TRIAL. BRING FLOWERS."

The music is somewhere else. Finding a place to rehearse has been a problem. Four amplified guitars, drums, and unlimited tambourines make a lot of noise, and the Group Image is kept on the run. Their prime time is after midnight. Minutes after they set up to rehearse the police usually arrive on a noise complaint. So they pack up and move again. They're resigned to the ritual. "Music is energy," one said. "You can get it in a different place but you can't stop it."

Nor has it been easy to find a place to perform. Their quest is for a home for survival in the country and a ballroom in the city. The ballroom is a great vision. The whole room would be wired for sound, not just the stage. "We'll work carbon dioxide exhaust pipes into the ballroom," one mused. "There are a lot of guys who want to play their motorcycles." They hope to keep admission at $1.00, but if you bring a tambourine you could probably get in the stage door. And join the Group Image.

Or you can join them now. "The Image isn't closed. We want other people to come and do their thing. We can give people an opportunity. It's lonely everywhere."

Or listen for rumors of their next appearance. Going to a Group Image hearing can be an engulfing experience. Like the Easter Be-In, you may be in for a surprise. The tribal spirit is contagious and it can catch you off guard. Be prepared to plunge in and feel what's happening.

YOUTHQUAKE

The Ukrainians had had enough.

"Hare Krishna" may be a song of love for the Lord Krishna, but it's a little esoteric for a Ukrainian grandmother who wants to sit in peace and talk about the old country. A daffodil is an empty gesture to an old man who can get no sleep at night. In the late afternoon on Memorial Day, the Flower People were out in force, complete with kirtan and bongoes, and some of the Ukrainians bitched to the park foreman.

The park foreman had had enough.

Tompkins Square had been a peaceful, if boring, park before the hippies came, and he had heard enough gripes from the Ukrainians to write a book. Moreover, the hippies were playing musical instruments, and sitting on the grass at that, both in violation of park regulations. He walked over to the Ninth Precinct station to make a noise complaint.

You can't ignore a formal complaint, so a couple of cops went over to the park and told the hippies to shut up and get off the grass. The kids laughed, and kept singing. The cops ordered them to leave. "They laughed at us," Patrolman John Rodd explained. "That's when the trouble started."

The cops had had enough.

A call went out for reinforcements, and three sergeants and fifteen patrolmen were sent to the park. By this time, the hippies had also been reinforced, and where there were once twenty hippies singing, there were now two hundred. The Tactical Patrol Force was summoned, and thirty-five radio cars and seventy riot-trained cops rushed to the scene. Again, they ordered the crowd to disperse.

The hippies had had enough.

They had been having a nice time, and Frank Wise had brought some groceries to pass around, and if they can't smoke grass in the park they can damn well sit on the grass and praise the Lord. They locked their arms and kept singing. And the cops started to pry them apart and carry them off to paddy wagons.

And Frank Wise had had enough.

Frank Wise is no kid. He is thirty-seven, working on a doctoral thesis, and his wife and infant child sat nearby as he rose to protest. "My God," he said, his arms outstretched as police dragged his friends away. "Where is this happening? This is America." A nightstick flew, and Frank Wise was covered with blood. More cops waded in, more nightsticks flew, and Wise became a martyr.

Bystanders wept, and everyone human should have gasped, my God, what has impatience wrought?

Wise was handcuffed and, bleeding from the ears, was taken away to a paddy wagon. Forty of his friends were jammed into three trucks. Hundreds followed the vans to the Ninth Precinct station on East 5th Street, and rallied outside to shout "fascists" and "murderers" at the gray stone walls. A half hour later, an ambulance arrived to take Wise and Tony di Stasi, who was also hit by nightsticks, to Bellevue Hospital. Wise refused treatment, and joined his friends for arraignment at the courthouse at 100 Centre Street.

At nine Tuesday night, when the prisoners were en route to night court, the Communications Company issued a mimeographed bulletin. The Communications Company, patterned after a successful Digger operation in San Francisco, was only a week old. Working out of the basement at Pablo on Bleecker Street, it had been set up precisely to deal with an emergency such as this: to get the word out in a crisis. The handbill told what happened in the park, announced a Be-In at Night Court, and gave subway instructions. Volunteers rushed to key locations in the Village to distribute it. The community responded. By ten the hall outside of Part 1A was teeming with hippies.

The entrance to the courtroom was blocked by a chain of TPF's and the kids paraded before them, in provocative splendor, complete with bells and bare feet. They sat underfoot to sing "Hare Krishna." They burned incense, and they carved what was perhaps the first watermelon to enter the hall of justice. Defiant, they slid down the bannisters. Determined, they posed in lotus position on the floors of telephone booths.

Behind a closed door, in the hallway that served as the cloakroom of the court, volunteer lawyers, reporters, cops, and city officials conferred on the crisis. Peter Aschkenasy and Courtney Callender trembled on behalf of the Parks Department, whose diligent Tompkins Square foreman, Emmanuel Kirschner, would soon repeat his complaint as plaintiff in the adjoining court. The East Side's own Bill Tatum, formerly with the Bolivar-Douglass Reform Club, now with the Department of Buildings, and immediately night mayor of the City of New York, strove to ease the situation. Attorney Ernst Rosenberger, noted recently for his defense of Ed Sanders and topless cellist Charlotte Moorman, prepared to represent the forty-one kids. When he had heard of the arrests, he had rushed to the courthouse in a borrowed tie and jacket to volunteer his services. In the hallway, he conferred with four other lawyers who had offered their help.

The defendants were brought in clusters before the judge over a period of four hours. They were still dressed for a picnic. Many wore beads and diffraction discs, some were barefoot, others had Day-glo paint on their hands and faces. Rosenberger introduced them as welfare workers, computer programers, college students and graduates, and fathers and mothers. Many of these charged with disorderly conduct were released on their own recognizance. Eight others were held on a total of $5,500 bail. By the next morning, after an all-night appeal on radio station WBAI, the bail was raised and only Frank Wise remained in jail.

The courtroom hushed when Wise was brought before Judge Vincent Rao shortly before midnight. It was incredible that he was conscious. He seemed dazed, his face gashed and beaten, his hair caked with blood. He braced himself against Rosenberger.

"I'd like the record to reflect the condition of the defendant," Rosenberger began, his voice choked with emotion. "There is a tear on his chin that is two inches long, a tear under his right eye that is three inches long."

The district attorney, a lady named Landau, asked that "the record reflect that the tear is a scratch." Wise glared at her. Their eyes met, and she turned away.

"The scratch is a quarter of an inch wide," Rosenberger said. "The defendant is married," he continued, "lives with his family, and has one child that is less than a year old."

Judge Rao looked up. "If he's got a wife and child at home," he asked, "then why is he out in the park, taking nightsticks away from police officers and striking them?"

Wise stiffened. "I have a hundred people who know what happened," he shouted. "I did none of these things. I have one hundred witnesses." Rosenberger tried to calm him as the judge rapped for order. Wise became docile. He had said what he had to.

Wise was charged with felonious assault on a police officer. Despite Rosenberger's efforts to have him released, Wise was remanded without bail because he had refused to be fingerprinted. On Thursday morning, he was released on $50.00 bond.

The following Tuesday, the kids returned to court. Only Wise remained charged with felonious assault. Four others were charged with simple assault. All forty-one were charged with disorderly conduct and interfering with an officer. The trial was postponed until June 27.

"If one more person comes up to me and says 'I've just talked with Captain Fink,'" a weary attorney said last week, "I'm going to slug him in the mouth."

Joseph Fink is commander of the Ninth Precinct. It is

widely believed that if he were on duty on Memorial Day, the melée would not have occurred. He was not, and he spent the rest of the week in an endless series of meetings and conferences in an attempt to repair the delicate good will, the prize of a year's tough work as chief on the Ninth, that had been shattered on Memorial Day. He met with clergymen, city officials, community leaders, and representatives of many hippie factions. Often there was a line in front of his small office on the ground floor of the station. In the course of the political aftermath of the Memorial Day mess, an audience with Fink came to be of some status. Hence the attorney's remark.

As city departments competed with self-absolutions and veiled accusations, the hippies emerged from the crisis as a community. They had won the park. The next day, the grassy battleground was designated a "troubador area" by Parks Commissioner August Heckscher, the gates were opened, and the "KEEP OFF THE GRASS" signs removed. The Communications Company, in a statement issued Wednesday afternoon, appealed for peace. "Let us make the result of the conflict be that the park has been opened to us. Let us accept the police as people in a gentle manner. They are civil servants and in that capacity let us love them."

The Group Image played to a packed park Wednesday night, but there were no cops around to love. Their absence was regretted later in the evening when a group of Puerto Rican youths, upset by the hippies' newly won dominance of the park, rained rocks and beer cans on the musicians. The Group Image made a hasty exit.

Meanwhile, at the Forum restaurant on Avenue A, a meeting was held to announce the formation of an East Village Defense Committee. Jim Nash, a former reporter for the *East Village Other,* attempted to describe the envisioned bureaucracy. It wasn't easy. The factions present at the Forum ranged from Black Mask militants to speed freaks, and their attention was clearly directed at Captain Fink who, invited to come as an observer, sat in the front row.

Nash stumbled through a list of the committee's ambitions. He sought a guarantee of proper police action. "What we mean by proper action," he explained sternly, "is what happened in the park was improper." He proposed a legal fund to aid "anyone in the East Village who has been harassed improperly." He proposed a twenty-four-hour communications system which, he suggested, "would also work with the mass media." Nash said that the committee would defend the residents of the East Village against improper entry. "The police have been entering the East Village illegally," he declared. Nash finally proposed a Maccabee-type patrol of the side streets on the East Side, and demanded the removal of the Tactical Patrol Force from the area.

The audience clamored for a chance at Fink. The captain rose to confront a barrage of angry questions and accusations.

"I couldn't possibly answer your questions," he began, "not because of how many but because of the type of questions they are. I came down to learn from you." He dodged a rain of loaded questions with blasé answers, and the anger of the audience quickly evolved into hysteria. The furious and the militant crushed forward with a chorus of accusations, and the meeting nearly became a riot. Fink was forced to leave. The militants were just getting warmed up, and the few Flower People in attendance emerged wilted.

June began on Thursday, and the Grateful Dead were in town and, despite some rumble rumors from the Puerto Ricans, the prospects for peace looked promising. A happy, scruffy parade of eighty marched down St. Mark's Place, complete with police escort, to present the Dead with a white carnation key to the East Village, graciously accepted by Pigpen. And the Tompkins Square bandshell rocked with San Francisco glory until a noise complaint was lodged in the late afternoon. Rather than tune down, the Dead turned off.

Thursday evening, ten people quietly gathered together around a low, candlelit table in the back room of the Family Store on East 6th Street. They represented many of the new tribes and communities of the East Side and the meeting, held at the request of the Communications Company, was New York's first tribal council. They had come together not to decide or lead or elect or demand, but simply to council: to explore a very old model of government that seemed to fit very new times. And they explored carefully and cautiously and candidly. They elected no leaders, nor did they plan to. They discussed the Communications Company, and agreed to support it. And they decided to meet again.

Later that night, the East Village Defense Committee met again, this time in a high-rise apartment on Charles Street, where the doorman could keep out the speed freaks. Nash stood in the corner, introduced the committee's press secretary, and began modestly: "For some crazy reason," he said, "I've been appointed chairman of all this." One of the kids who was arrested recounted the Memorial Day incident. Then the committee got down to business. They were anxious to help. They would set up a bail fund, a legal fund, and could handle the press. Some visitors from the East Side explained that the Jade Companions had a bail fund in operation, that the Communications Company had a phone functioning, and that several lawyers had been working for months without a sponsoring organization. Perhaps the East Village Defense Committee could join these groups.

Several lawyers present adjourned to the kitchen.

Abbie Hoffman was sitting on the floor. "We had a good thing going on the East Side," he said. "The groups were stumbling along. I think that this committee could do a real service to the community by disbanding." He grinned. "Think of it," he exclaimed. "A committee disbanding after two days. It'd be a whole turn in American political life."

Nash smiled. "Abbie," he said. "No."

Then the meeting became a little confused. The storefront was available, it seems, but had not yet been rented. But the Communications Company could use it, and Jim Fouratt agreed that they could certainly use a storefront. So the hat was passed to pay for the committee's headquarters. And when they moved into the store they could get a phone, or perhaps an answering service, but Olivia had a phone in her store, and why have an answering service when her phone could be used.

The lawyers returned from the kitchen. They announced that they had decided to join together for the legal defense of the hippies. They would seek other lawyers, and set up a rotating system where each lawyer would be available for a week at a time. But they felt that the lawyers' group should remain independent of any other organization. It was a breakthrough.

But the emergency telephone plagued the meeting. There was a dispute over whether it should start that night, with a temporary number at Olivia's, or whether they should hold off until a permanent number could be found. Should the temporary number be publicized, or would it then be confused when a permanent number was set up? It was tossed back and forth for half an hour. Olivia offered to man the phone until eight in the morning, and everyone wrote down the number.

Meanwhile, the Tactical Patrol Force was back in Tompkins Square Park.

All day there were rumors that the Puerto Ricans were up-tight. The rumors were true. They knew about Memorial Day, and they had heard the "LSD music" and they thought that the hippies were taking over the park. The park was tense Thursday night as the Pageant Players performed three antiwar plays. "There was some hostile response," Michael Brown of the Pageant Players recalled, "but there always is when we perform in the street. The last thing we tried was an improvisation about the events in the park Tuesday. At the end of it, there was a small fight in the audience."

The Pageant Players were followed by a folk-rock group, and a group of Puerto Ricans came to the bandshell and demanded Latin music. Some words were exchanged, and a scuffle started, and the iron curtain was pulled down to close the stage.

The kids then moved to Hoving's Hill, knocked over a couple of sanitation barrels, and began to work on a Latin beat. A tall blonde, Wendy Allen, went up to protest. The kids attacked her and tore her clothes. A mob formed around her and hurtled toward the park entrance at East 7th Street and Avenue B. There, a police sergeant rescued her and summoned reinforcements.

The mob, rapidly growing, milled in the intersection. Some jumped atop cars, crushing the roofs. A motorcyclist came toward the intersection. He was pulled off his bike, and the cycle was disintegrated. At 10:15 p.m. reinforcements from the Ninth Precinct arrived. They took positions and waited, taunted by the kids.

By eleven, Chief Inspector Garelick and Police Commissioner Leary were on the scene, and shortly thereafter a force of TPF and motorcycle cops began to disperse the crowd. The mob disappeared into the side streets. Police then sealed off Tompkins Square Park for the night.

The Puerto Ricans had had enough.

Late that night, around three in the morning, a small group of Puerto Ricans and a small group of hippies met together in the basement of Pablo to try to prevent another Watts. They had planned to put out a bilingual handbill to calm the neighborhood. At first they were going to say, "Mothers, keep your children at home."

But they talked some more and decided there was a better way. Instead of having no music that night, they would have music all day. They would pass out armbands, and tell the people they were *Serenos* or peacekeepers. They would pass out armbands to everyone who would take one, and tell them to link arms and surround any trouble. And what *Sereno* would ever start a fight? At four in the morning, they telephoned Captain Fink and the Department of Parks and the night mayor, Holt Meyer.

They talked with Meyer for almost an hour, and pleaded for an appointment with Lindsay. He was skeptical, but he told them to come down and wait in the lobby of City Hall.

They arrived at City Hall at nine. A half-hour later, they met with James L. Marcus, Commissioner of Water Supply, Gas, and Electricity, who represented the mayor, and Meyer, the previous night's mayor; Peter Aschkenasy, deputy police commissioner for community relations; and Captain Fink, whom they had invited. They talked until noon, and the City agreed with their plans.

As they left the meeting on the second floor of City Hall, they met a wall of newsmen. The kids refused to comment or identify themselves. "We're not leaders," one said. "We're just some people who got together."

As they left City Hall, a mob of landlords strained at the police barricades. They were shouting something about hippies. Vito Battista, chairman of the United Taxpayers Party, screamed into the microphone, "Lindsay sees the hippies, but he won't see the taxpayers." As the kids disappeared around the corner, the landlords stormed City Hall. Rocks crashed through the windows. Lindsay later disclaimed any knowledge of the meeting.

That afternoon, the Communications Company went bilingual. "Tonight," the mimeographed sheet read, "we will have music in Tompkins Square Park. Also if you have any problems please speak with the *Serenos*, who will be wearing white armbands on their right arms. We don't need a lot of police here tonight."

The park was jammed Friday night. Mongo Santamaria played, and Len Chandler sang, and Chino Garcia from the Real Great Society mc'd in Spanish. The *Serenos* were everywhere, even though some wore the armbands on their heads as dew-rags, the uniform of a rumble. Even the police were there, but you wouldn't recognize them unless you saw the paper clips on their lapels. Hippies and Puerto Ricans together grooved on the Latin music.

And when the music stopped shortly before midnight, everyone held his breath. But there was no riot.

Captain Fink later praised the *Serenos*. "I'm very happy we had the cooperation of the *Serenos*," he said. "If more community people would show an interest in the situation, I'm sure that this would prevent further incidents from happening in this area."

Saturday afternoon the Fugs played in the bandshell, and tourists swarmed into the park. That evening, Ronald Komer, a *Daily News* employee, was walking across the grass. He tripped over some Puerto Ricans, and some words were exchanged, and Komer was slashed across the stomach with a knife. Komer was taken to Bellevue Hospital, where he was in satisfactory condition, and Gilberto Concepcion, seventeen, was taken to jail.

"Gilberto Concepcion is in trouble," read the Communications Company bulletin later that night. "Help raise bail for 17-year-old Gilberto being held in stabbing of *Daily News* reporter Ronald Komer in Tompkins Square Park last night. Gilberto needs the help of the community. He needs our help now, not the Tombs."

By Tuesday they had raised $500.00.

Komer could have been stabbed on Christmas morning on Avenue C because he didn't know the mores of the Lower East Side, the first one being that you never insult a Puerto Rican. The tourists were coming en masse to watch the action, but they were more likely to start it.

The community rallied to discourage the tourists, and Sunday the bandshell was closed. Monday, Parks Commissioner August Heckscher called a meeting of representatives of the various neighborhood groups and, backed by a consensus at the meeting, he revoked a permit issued to the New East Village Association for a four-month series of concerts in the bandshell. It was felt that the concerts attracted tourists, but were not representative enough to satisfy the community.

By Tuesday, Tompkins Square Park was calm, and half of the Lower East Side was involved in meetings, well laced with power politics. Many of the hippies in the other half wished that Emmett Grogan, the Jesus of the Diggers, were back in town. Because he understood these things. He had landed in New York in March and rocked the East Side with a lot of lessons he had learned in San Francisco. He had said to turn on to the Puerto Ricans and fuck the leaders. But a lot of people forgot what he said.

THE *SERENOS*

The girl burst into the storefront of the Visiting Mothers, like a guerrilla into a nursery.

"There's going to be some trouble in the park," she said. She paused to catch her breath. "The kids in the park are really up-tight."

Riots had almost become routine for Linda Cusamano. "We've got to get the *Serenos*," she said. She went to the kitchen and began to rummage around for the white armbands which have become the symbol of armistice on the East Side.

Linda Cusamano returned to the room with an armful of sheets torn into strips. She passed them out, tied one on her right arm, and began to walk toward Tompkins Square Park. On the way, she paused to talk to kids standing in the doorways of the tenements, taking the temperature of the street.

A large crowd had gathered around the bandshell in the park. Enclosed by a sea of heads were several rows of benches filled with a rather elegant audience which had come that warm spring evening to enjoy a classical recital. On the edge of the crowd, the kids were restless. The Puerto Ricans are down on long hair, whether Haydn or hippie.

A tight pack of twelve kids had been roaming the park. Now they stood next to the crowd. Linda Cusamano went up to them, and they talked vigorously for a few minutes. They knew her. They had seen her every day on the street.

The kids split, to continue roaming through the mazes of Tompkins Square. "They're not telling me anything," she laughed. But every few minutes, like a cold-war diplomat, she would approach them again and they would talk some more.

She had passed out the armbands to a new corps of *Serenos*. All that went with the uniform was a name and instructions to link arms and surround any trouble. But, despite the rumors, when the recital ended at 11 p.m. the park seemed well below the riot threshold.

The steel mesh screen rattled down over the bandshell. The audience ambled to the west. The kids stampeded to the east. And Linda Cusamano returned to the Visiting Mothers storefront.

By two in the morning, 10th Street was quiet. Quiet

enough so that Linda Cusamano could leave to go to WBAI for an all-night bail appeal. A kid from 10th Street was in jail, and she needed him. He had been at her side for a week, throughout all the turmoil in Tompkins Square, talking and getting people together and talking some more. A few days later he was busted by narcotics police.

The bail was raised, and by ten in the morning Linda Cusamano was in court, gloves in hand, to see him released. Now, while he is awaiting trial, he is working full-time for Visiting Mothers.

At noon, Linda Cusamano returned to the storefront. It was full of children now, left in the care of mothers on welfare while other mothers went to work or search for work.

She went to the back room, which is her home, to sleep.

Linda Cusamano is a teacher. She is teaching people how to survive in the city. She has little use for the Horatio Alger fantasies that so often inspire the professional social worker. Horatio Alger was a freak. The escapee is no help to the inmate. The success story is a television cliché to the kids on Avenue C, and high school equivalency tests are a drag. Bail when they're busted is something else.

She is working in the meantime, before the long-range goals of the vocational training-remedial education programs are realized. She is moved by the families that fall apart in the meantime, by the mothers who give up their babies for lack of immediate relief. With armbands and milk and a few friends from the street, Linda Cusamano is hacking at the here and now.

She knows what she's up against. She is pretty and

twenty-two and has lived on the Lower East Side all her life. She hasn't been through it; she is still in it. She dropped out of Seward Park High School in the tenth grade, and has never been rehabilitated. She has trouble with progress reports, but she talks beautifully and eloquently. And some of the City's most powerful officials come by the storefront to listen, because Linda Cusamano knows the Lower East Side.

Visiting Mothers began as a salvage operation after an ambitious plan for a Lower East Side Day-Care Center was rejected by the Federal Welfare Administration a year ago. Linda envisioned a day-care center to relieve mothers of infant children so they could work, look for work, take advantage of opportunities offered by the poverty program, or simply shop for groceries. Without such crèche services, as are available throughout Europe for working mothers, many mothers face no alternative but to give up children to foster homes or go on welfare. The Welfare Administration praised her efforts, but declined the funds. A year ago, Linda joined with the Real Great Society, a self-help organization of former gang members financed by a grant from the Astor Foundation, and opened a storefront at 370 East 10th Street. But it was an uneasy alliance and on June 12 they parted ways. Now Linda is desperate for funds for the summer.

The day-care service is the nucleus of Visiting Mothers. At eight each weekday morning, the storefront opens to receive children of working mothers who pay $15.00 a week for the service. The children are cared for by mothers on welfare, who work full time for $30.00 a week. Now it's a hand-to-mouth operation. The working mothers bring milk and cookies, and lunch has lately been bologna sandwiches. A few weeks ago, Visiting Mothers ran out of milk. WBAI responded with an all-night "Milk-In" on the Bob Fass Show. "We had milk in every freezer on 10th Street," Linda recalled.

But the Visiting Mothers do more than day-care. When tension in the Puerto Rican community reached the riot level several weeks ago, Linda conceived the *Serenos*. While the Tactical Patrol Force was still in Tompkins Square Park, Linda was on the phone to City Hall pleading for a chance to test the idea. She worked through the night and through the next day, talking with city officials and, with her friend Carmen Mateos, talking with the kids in the street. The next night, hundreds of people in Tompkins Square Park wore the white armbands, ready to join together to stop any trouble, and the riot that seemed inevitable never materialized.

Linda spends a lot of time in the street. Like any kid on the Lower East Side, she knows her block and she's proud of it. And the kids on the block know her. With a lot of respect for native knowledge, she has bridged the communications barrier that plagues the social worker who commutes to the slums. "I've got a good thing going with these kids," she said. "They never call me cop. They'd like to, but I'm on the street all the time. They see me. The kids that were really involved that night have been coming around to the storefront and we sit and drink beer and play guitar. They are really into a beautiful music thing.

"The kids down here are very alert," she said. "And they're sharp and they're smart. Don't tell me about high school equivalency tests. The kids don't want to be tied down to training programs. They want to work with things that will immediately affect their lives."

Immediately. A girl comes to the storefront late in the evening. She is out of money and her baby sister needs milk. Linda goes to the kitchen and gives her a quart. Immediately. The park is tense and mothers tear sheets into armbands. Immediately. A kid from 10th Street is busted and Linda Cusamano is out raising bail.

"I want people to learn to live in the city," she said. "They've got to accept the fact that they're going to be here for a while and make it better."

Her vision is a series of block centers which would encompass day-care, a twenty-four-hour communications service, workshops, job listings, small apartment repairs, health services, musical instruction, a bail fund, the *Serenos,* and a diaper service. It's not as ponderous as it sounds. The musical instruction, Linda explained, could be on stoops and in laundromats, "just to teach them a little bit more than they know."

The idea of a bail fund is now being tested by the hippie community. Linda likes it. "We need a bail fund for every block," she said. "I don't care what the rap is. Everybody should be out on bail. They could parole kids to the block center, and demote some of this absurd ego thing that's going on.

"The hippies could teach the kids carpentry," she mused. "They're good at that. They could show them how to build aerial beds, and then there would be a lot more room. The tenants could work with the landlords to renovate the buildings. Can you imagine? Eventually landlords might be hiring crews of these kids.

"You teach the kids carpentry in the city, and the next year take them to the country to build domes."

Domes in the country are an important part of Linda's vision. She feels that relief in the country is essential to survival in the city. She is already looking for land out of the city where families could stay for two weeks this summer. Next summer she hopes to have kids from the East Side assembling low-cost geodesic domes, which they could sell in the winter when they return to the city.

"We'll call it Camp *Sereno*," she said.

Meanwhile, the rent is due on the storefront and the frozen milk is nearly finished. Her funds were cut off in mid-June and it is now too late to apply for summer grants. Without some relief, without food or rent or minimal salaries, Visiting Mothers may have to close.

"I'm lost," she said quietly. "I need somebody to hold the ladder. I need people to stand behind me while I'm in the street.

"What are we? We're women in the community who are doing more than isolating our miseries."

COUNTRY JOE AND THE FISH

They landed at Stony Brook. It wasn't a large turnout for the first East Coast concert of Country Joe and the Fish. It seemed that half the audience was the Group Image, and they could dance unhindered across the vast courts of the gymnasium of the State University. It was night, and the electric music wafted across the cool dark fields of the campus. Country Joe sounds best in the country, where the air is clear: on a highway near Big Sur with bonfires for light, on the meadows of a mountain in

Marin County. The sound depends on precision, and there are fewer flaws in the fields.

They are a Berkeley band, and first came together two years ago around a coffeehouse called the Jabberwock. Then Joe McDonald and Barry Melton were into jug-band music, and the group began to form around them. "When the Jabberwock needed a jug band," Joe recalls, "we were the jug band. When they needed a songwriter, I was the songwriter. When they needed a comedy act, Barry was the comedy act." They gradually went to work in the San Francisco dance halls, which were then at their peak. Their reputation spread, their sound became tighter, and they began to tour the dance halls of the Coast: Vancouver, Portland, Seattle, Santa Barbara. They played at be-ins and benefits. In 1966 they cut their first single, "Rag Baby"; and six months ago their first album came out on Vanguard. Now Country Joe had come to the City, and the Stony Brook concert was a gentle transition.

If there is a theme to their music, it is what's inside changing order. They are bards, in a sense, spreading the word about a new era, or proclaiming a comic book obituary to the old. Some in simple fantasy. "I'm stuck on the L.A. freeway, rainwater in my boots. . . . Up come two cats in a Cadillac and they say won't you hop in, man. I went flying high all the way." Some is topical, and the ugliness of the old order gets the ax. "Come out Lyndon with your hands held high. Drop your guns, baby, and reach for the sky. Got you surrounded, you ain't got a chance. Send you back to Texas, make you work on your ranch." And then, as an afterthought, "make him eat flowers" and "make him drop some acid." The latter afterthought was erased on monaural, but it survived on stereo.

They sing about the I-Ching, and they sing about acid, flawless sounds about flawless trips, and they sing an occasional sweet melancholy ballad about the fading past, and they sing apocalyptic visions of the future. The visions unfold like a sunrise, when David Cohen's organ eclipses into silence and re-enters as dawn.

At their best, they seem to be toying with pure energy. Then the listener, the communicant, can understand that Country Joe and the Fish play "electric music" as opposed to rock. Country Joe's voice seems to dance on the waves of energy which emanate from the amplifiers. The myriad chords of the guitars suddenly come together and explode again. Their compositions can be mystical. Some could be a score for Blake.

The novice to rock is most often put off by the amplification. At times it is justified. Amplification only for a sensation is a ruse. It is no more impressive (and far more oppressive) than any other gimmick. But when the equipment is good and the compositions are sophisticated and the group is together, amplification turns the concert into a total experience. Thus it is with Country Joe and the Fish. They cannot be background music.

Hand in hand with the energy of the music are the lights. The Union Light Company, who first played with Country Joe at the Eagles' Auditorium in Seattle, came to New York with fifteen projectors in an old hearse to appear with the group at the Cafe Au Go Go. They developed in isolation in Seattle, but their lights are equal to the best in New York. A wall of light is orchestrated into movements. A huge mandala rolls the length of the wall over a dozen different shimmering spectacles. Pictures quietly appear—antique slides of Indian chiefs, a benign Ho Chi Minh—and then submerge into patterns. Lights are important to Country Joe, although strobes will do in a pinch.

Like the world they sing about, Country Joe and the Fish are still in the process of developing and now have to learn how to deal with success. They are part of that world, a world which demands and imposes a constant self-scrutiny of motives and profits. In the music business, they must meet with another world that they once escaped, and New York, so the story goes among rock circles on the West Coast, is the epitome of that world. The Fish were tense last week.

They try to remain close to their own world, as their own world is close to them. Their album has been a soundtrack for countless trips. In a gag interruption they promote their "alternate sponsor: the manufacturers and distributors of LSD-25." Like most Coast groups, they play free concerts, to remain accessible to their audience as concert prices soar.

Last Saturday, they played to an audience of several thousand in Tompkins Square Park. Although they were plagued by bad equipment, as they have been since they arrived, the audience was stoned enough to dig it. Simultaneously, another Smoke-In was held. As Joe sang "Hey, partner, won't you pass that reefer round," the lead into "Bass String," a ten-year-old kid passed me a joint. Later, a carton of buttons was hurled into the air (mostly reading "PRAY FOR SEX"). It was a good free day.

If the free concerts are a relief for the group, a sort of vestige of the days when the Avalon and the Fillmore were young and the Trips Festival a fresh memory, the paid appearances can be oppressive. "You're like a minstrel show," Barry Melton explains. "It's like you're in blackface. You're playing to people who came to see you as freaks and they don't really like you." But Joe is optimistic.

"When we first got together," he said, "we were all misfits. Now we're emerging as a group.

"We're going to make mistakes. We're a friendly band. We're amusing. But when we're terrible, we're really terrible."

True enough. But when they're good, they're out of sight.

COPS PLEAD: "KEEP OFF THE GRASS"

Mayor Lindsay missed the major sights in his tour of Tompkins Square Park Monday night. Unlike the frequent tourist, he didn't scale Hoving's Hill, he didn't walk on the liberated grass, and he shunned the site in front of the bandshell where early this summer mobs rose and ebbed and where more recently grass has enjoyed a rare sanctuary.

He did pace around the outer walk of the park, with neighborhood kids under his feet, Joe Louis and newly promoted Deputy Inspector Joseph Fink at his side, and a large cross-section of the East Side neighborhood hurtling along behind.

The mayor's visit was a climax to another tense week in the park. His appearance was a relief to kids in front of the bandshell, who had been unable to explain the presence of an unusually large number of plainclothesmen and uniformed cops.

The park had seemed a sanctum, like Millbrook, for several weeks. In early August, with the encouragement of New York Provo, hippies and Puerto Ricans came together on a Sunday afternoon to share a pipe of peace. The first Smoke-In was a success. At least no one was busted, and the next weekend no advertisements were necessary for a concert of Country Joe and the Fish. Then, as joints were passed like a bottle of wine on the Bowery, precedent seemed established. In the following weeks, visitors from Haight-Ashbury were impressed with New York as never before. Paranoia took a plunge, and grass was in open evidence at demonstrations on St. Mark's Place, Group Image functions, and various gentle gatherings.

It was the same last Saturday. You couldn't tell the smoke from the smog. Residents passed joints to astounded tourists, and there wasn't a uniformed cop in sight. As dusk fell, the audience stumbled stoned out of the park.

It was too good. That evening, after burning rubbish for hours in defiance of the police, vandals made a bonfire of six park benches. Sunday afternoon, narcotics police in plain clothes arrested three people in front of the bandshell after the kids allegedly offered the cops a joint.

The police took Barbara Young, Donald Kingsley, and Michael Werkhoven to the Ninth Precinct station, where they were booked for offering a marijuana cigarette to a police officer. A hundred people from the park followed them to the station, and demonstrated outside for an hour. A kid with a guitar sang a long, funny ballad about the City and the mayor and the cops. Police observed from nearby rooftops. And even in the front yard of the Ninth Precinct station, an occasional joint was shared.

The crowd followed their comrades to the courthouse. They waited an hour on the steps before court convened, and, yea, even in the shadow of the Tombs the brave lit up.

They packed the otherwise empty courtroom as their friends came before the judge. The defendants, who were represented by Legal Aid, were released without bail. Now the press waited on the steps of the courthouse, and the kids blew grass for the cameras. Michael Werkhoven, one of the arrested, told CBS that "God is really alive," and as the kid with the guitar began to sing his funny ballad to network television, a purist recoiled.

"Don't do a minstrel show for them," he snarled, and collared the kid. The ballad ended abruptly. "What are you, crazy? Some kind of nut?" The purist left and the ballad resumed.

Then the crowd, elated with victory, marched up the Bowery and back to the park.

But the pax pot was no more and the paranoia pox had returned. The kids bemoaned the short-lived sanctum, and at one point in the mayor's whirlwind visit surrounded him, chanting "We Want Pot." Lindsay kept his smile.

The kids credit Deputy Inspector Fink for the tolerance that prevailed for several weeks, a credit which Fink neither desires nor deserves. Fink, who was just promoted from Captain to Deputy Inspector (under a new department policy, he will remain in command of the Ninth Precinct despite the promotion), cites several arrests by both Ninth Precinct police and narcotics officers that went unnoticed by the community during the supposed truce. "They started with banana hash in the park," he said. "They then moved on to oregano, turkish tobacco, and pot incense. Now they are progressing to grass, and some will get busted."

Citing the letter of the marijuana laws, Fink explained that offering grass was a felony as well as selling it. "You know," he said, "when they're standing in a circle passing a joint around, if they hold the butt it's a misdemeanor. When they give it to another person, it's a felony."

New York Provo, which has its headquarters in a storefront at 197 Avenue A, attributes the crackdown to the burning of the park benches. "A few people wanted to bait the police," a Provo handbill declared. "They blew our cool by burning things other than grass." Provo is now attempting to organize park patrons in self-defense. The handbills urge demonstrations after busts, and offer to "print pictures of bonafide undercover agents."

But relations between the neighborhood and the Ninth Precinct remain warm. The Diggers recently invited the patrolmen of the Ninth and their families to a picnic. Fink has asked for volunteers, slow to come, and a tentative date has been set around Labor Day. Fink only asks that the hosts keep off the grass. "Cops are on duty twenty-four hours a day," he said. "If the kids start smoking grass, they'll have to bust them. Maybe they can bring banana hash instead."

THE DIGGERS DIG A TREE

Two weeks ago, the Diggers closed St. Mark's Place to traffic. So last Saturday, riding the momentum of the madness, they decided to plant a tree.

First they needed a tree. So after dark the night before, four Diggers and a dog piled into a Volkswagen bus. They rounded the first corner on two wheels and bombed down Broadway to the Staten Island Ferry.

The dog vaulted the seats in the bus. "What's the dog for?" Abbie asked.

"If he pisses on the tree, it's a good one," Rich said.

They boarded a ferry. "It's like a warship," Abbie said. "Don't you feel like you're going to war?"

Rich climbed the yardarms of the car deck, hand over his eyes, peering toward Staten Island like a pirate.

In a few minutes they had arrived at Staten Island. They piled back in the bus. Rich gunned it across the ramp, drove two blocks, and circled around toward the waterfront, eyeing the shrubbery in a vacant lot.

"Those trees are no good, Rich. They're weed trees."

Three parks and two front yards later, they had arrived at the closest thing to country in the City. The bus hurtled across a field in a two-rut trail, the headlights bouncing in the night, and slid to a halt in the tall grass in the middle of the field.

"No trees, but we can get dirt," Rich said. The dog bounded through the grass. Rich chopped at the cement soil with a hoe. And Abbie fell in a pit.

In a few minutes they were back on the road. The bus was pulled up on the soft clay of the shoulder, which Rich was furiously transplanting into the back of the bus. He filled five boxes, and then began to shovel soil on top of them.

The dog was back in the grass. "There's a tree," Abbie shouted. He slid down the dark embankment into the grass, and fell in the swamp.

So the bus was full of dirt to fertilize St. Mark's Place, but still they needed a tree. Less than a mile away, alone in a vacant lot, grew a little fifteen-foot oak sapling— the kind you see in advertisements in magazines. They found it.

"A perfect tree," they shouted, and began to dig. With an Army shovel and hoe, the Diggers dug a hole around the roots of the tree. The tree trembled. "Leave some roots, Rich," Abbie said. "It's gotta live." The tree shuddered. They dug three feet into the ground, and Rich took the hatchet and . . . and . . .

"It's got enough roots," he said.

"Now how are we gonna get it into the truck?" Abbie asked. "It's bigger than the truck."

The bus looked like a greenhouse as the Diggers drove back to the ferry. Passing motorists leaned out their windows to cheer. The roots grazed the dashboard, the top bent around the rear window, and the Diggers peered through the lush foliage.

"How much for the tree?" they asked the ferryman.

"Trees are free." He had the idea.

And they brought it back to the City, to keep for the

night in the back yard of the Communications Company. All night they watered the little oak, with a hose rigged up from the kitchen.

Saturday night, the Diggers planted a fir in a mound of dirt in St. Mark's Place. Alas, the little oak had pined away.

The street was closed to traffic, and the Group Image, plugged into the current of the East Side Book Store, played to the crowd of three thousand. They were set up on top of a huge flatbed truck. Abbie stood on one corner of the truck, holding up a sign which read "ONLY GOD CAN MAKE A TREE." Rich stood on the other corner, burning dollar bills. The Group Image began to play "Dancing in the Streets," and the crowd swayed, dodging a few eggs which were thrown from tenement windows. Benign cops strolled through the crowd, breathing the smoke-filled air. Soon a rain of yogurt overwhelmed the eggs. The yogurt people goofed, and donated five hundred containers of strawberry yogurt labeled raspberry, to the Diggers. Little of the yogurt was consumed. The containers were opened and the contents hurled into the crowd. Some had umbrellas. Others weren't so lucky.

At the end of the dance, Police Captain Fink walked to the tree and uprooted it with a yank. The crowd moaned. Bob Fass rushed forward to save the tree, which Fink gladly relinquished, and led a parade to Tompkins Square Park where the tree was planted on the peak of Hoving's Hill.

And there it stands today, slightly tilting, at the highest point in the park.

THE FREE STORE

The one rule was "No Stealing."

Aside from that, it was a free-for-all from the moment the Diggers opened the doors to the Free Store Thursday night. Even when the storefront, at 264 East 10th Street, had filled to capacity, there were still hundreds of people stretched along the block, leaning on cars and drinking free coffee which was given away on the sidewalk. As people moved from the store to the street, space opened up bit by bit. A few entered, a few left, and when the piles of clothing lay scattered on the floor, the Diggers would hold the door shut for a few minutes while helpers stacked and redistributed the wealth.

Would the impact on New York be instant? Would mottoes ("We cannot be undersold") and values become obsolete? For once the Diggers hoped the Establishment would seek to exploit a good thing. The uptown stores have had Be-Ins, said one Digger. "Now let them have a free day!"

"It's interesting," said Paul Goodman, who was stacking clothes. "It sets your mind going."

A free store has been a goal of organized heads on the East Side since the idea was first kindled by Digger emissaries from Haight-Ashbury in the spring. When the wheels were finally set in motion, it took four days from signing the lease and turning the key to opening the store. In those four days, the Diggers, with a lot of help from their friends, painted the walls, built the shelves, put up a Day-glo façade, and stocked the store with five truckloads of clothes, quickly depleted and quickly replenished. The stock came in as fast as it left—quite a trick for a free store. "Friday someone came down and gave away a motorcycle," a Digger said. "And a newcomer—a kid who just arrived from the Midwest—left his suitcase, with all his clothes and shaving stuff and everything. He said we could have it."

The store is total theater. For the hippies it was no surprise, for the kids it was natural, and for the old people native to the East Side it was strange. An old lady tried on a hat and complained that it didn't fit her. The Diggers told her that her size would be in next week.

"This is like an energy exchange," a girl named Morning Dove explained, "and the energy is in flowers and clothes and pots and pans."

The audience freaked out the first night. Neighborhood kids, who never had a grandmother's attic, stumbled around in secondhand dresses and high heels. "Don't people take a lot of things they don't need?" a man asked a Digger. "It's a sale," the Digger replied, "and people take a lot of things they don't need at sales. But after the sale it will be business as usual."

A bearded hippie walked out in a silk smoking jacket. He said he was going to use it as a smoking jacket.

A sign read: "IF YOU BREAK IT, YOU'VE GOT TO TAKE IT."

Free stores have been thriving in San Francisco for over a year. A successful schism resulted in the Black Man's Free Store in the Fillmore ghetto. Though New York is a rough place to put it over, it looks as if it will work.

In the back of the store, the Diggers are already cooking free stew, which they give out daily at 4 p.m. in Tompkins Square Park. "The prayer meeting is the food," said a Digger in reference to some of the more conventional, competing facilities of the Lower East Side.

The Diggers' next goal is a free medical clinic, and several doctors have already offered their services. They plan to open offices on St. Mark's Place, with legal aid and housing and job referral services. "We'll come up with that in a few weeks if we get some funds," a Digger said.

In the meantime, Allen Ginsberg will find an answer waiting when he gets back from Europe to a question he asked in a poem in *Howl*, published in 1956.

"When can I go into the supermarket and buy what I need with my good looks?" Ginsberg asked.

The answer is now.

THE STREET IS THEATER

Normally it wouldn't be tolerated. There are laws against littering the sidewalk if not the air and, as a guard gruffly explained, the ink-stained yellow flowers which sagged like a limp wreath from the ledge above the Consolidated Edison lobby door were "defacing private property." But the guard didn't take them down. When the soot hit the fan he huddled with the others in the lobby, safe from the freaks on the Irving Place sidewalk.

It was Black Flower Day, unexpected, unannounced, and neither the press nor the police were invited. Suddenly there they were, several Diggers, clowns, and friends, gathered around a striking banner which declared "BREATHING IS BAD FOR YOUR HEALTH." Around 4:30 p.m. Wednesday they began to pass out flowers on Irving Place, or, rather, push flowers. It was a pushy demonstration, a novel thing, not a picket line cordoned by cops that a bystander could sneer at, but the kind of thing you admire or avoid. The Diggers offered the blackened mums with a sort of "take this flower and shove it" smirk. Secretaries scurried off.

It began with the flowers and evolved to handfuls of soot which made quick gray clouds in the air. When the soot appeared, the traffic in and out of the twenty-six-story office building came to a halt. The lobby jammed, and when a man in a suit came to the sidewalk to angrily close the doors, he did so in a cloud of black dust. Splotches of soot soiled his white shirt and bald head and the Diggers roared with laughter.

Con Ed was under siege. A clown pranced up and down the sidewalk. A costumed youth sprayed mist out of a vintage Flit can. The Diggers danced over a carpet of stained yellow petals, laughing and throwing soot in the air. Not that they looked dangerous (although several had a Hell's Angels aura) but they were weird. A confrontation promised to be embarrassing. So Con Ed called the cops, and wished the Diggers would leave. Save for a few maverick secretaries, who risked the wrath of the great generators by laughing, Con Ed stayed under cover.

By the time the police arrived, the Diggers had lit

several smoke flares upwind from the doors and split. Great clouds of smoke left a film on the face of the building. And only after the police had arrived did many feel it was safe to leave the lobby.

It was classic street theater, a Digger drama improvised with the idea that a handful of soot down an executive's neck might be more effective than a pile of petitions begging for cleaner air. Even at the sacrifice of good will, the gesture cannot be ignored. It will be remembered, long after the deaths during periods of high pollution are passed off as asthma attacks. The medium is the message. Such a versatile phrase.

Street theater has been copy for the front pages of the *San Francisco Chronicle* for over a year. The Diggers in San Francisco, many of whom are professional actors in the San Francisco Mime Troupe, are clever masters of media. Clever like butchering a horse at the gates of San Quentin to protest an execution. Clever like bringing flutes to the steps of City Hall for an anti-rat demonstration. They saw the power of the penny whistle. The simplest prop can unite a crowd for no reason at all. They sought the autonomy to stand on a street corner for an hour or a week. They introduced free food—food so free that you don't even have to eat it. Free to bury in the ground or rub in your face or feed to your dog or fertilize a tree. Free cream pies aren't meant to be eaten. It would be a waste. The Diggers declared war on conditioned responses. They blew minds by breaking subtle mores. They practiced public nuisance.

Digger emissaries from the Haight began to appear in Manhattan last spring. They were received in the hippie community like visiting royalty. They rapped to a series of meetings about free stores and fucking the leaders and

turning-on Puerto Ricans, but between their visits the
momentum would die and the torch would be snuffed.
The organization of the hippie community began at every
meeting for months, but it was rarely continued, which
may have been a blessing. For all the hopes of ESSO
(East Side Service Organization) and the Jade Companions, the Tribal Council and the block committees, the
East Village Defense Committee and the Gallery Gwen, a
shower of Digger dollars off the balcony of the New York
Stock Exchange seemed the most significant development
in months.

Free money is a cinch. It is the surest act in the Digger
repertoire. Any scruffy hippie who lights a match to a
dollar bill is guaranteed a response. The bystander will
inevitably react, thus losing his immunity as a bystander,
which is the goal. Furthermore, with a little planning the
press will be available to expand the audience, although
that audience is secure behind the glass of the evening
news, for on television, street theater becomes straight
theater: a rerun at best.

The press may even expand the act. The recent "ex-
posé" of Jim Fouratt in the *Daily News* could be, from a
Digger point of view, a blessing in admirable disguise. It
is one thing when some hippie burns or eats or throws
away his own money. It's guaranteed to raise a smile. But
the *News* revealed that Fouratt is a ward of the taxpayer.
That wasn't his allowance he had stuffed in his mouth, the
News reader notes with horror. It was at once a City
salary and home relief from the Welfare Department. The
freak is complete.

Thus were the Diggers introduced to New York. To
drive the point home, last Friday they burned more
money on the doorstep of the *Daily News*. And Saturday

several Diggers showed up at the Socialist Scholars' Conference at the Hilton to fire cap pistols at the bewildered politicos. Strange things should be happening on the streets of New York until the media bores. Manhattan is becoming a certified stage.

Of course, it is only the intention that is new. New York, far more than San Francisco, has always been a stage. Even a stray hippie outside his East Side sanctuary is cast in a role. Madison Avenue is a stage for a male hippie in flower. An audience is inevitable. He will react to the audience and the audience will react to him. If both are aware of it, the act is complete. He could hold up a mirror to drive the point home. Finally, as the Diggers say themselves, the street *is* theater. Countless acts on every corner: the panhandler, the prostitute, the poodle, the police. Recognition is the key.

PART TWO

"I've been looking in closets trying to find me," he said. "And that's what I'm doing now. I'm not sure if I like what I see."

He took a hand mirror and held it under the desk lamp. And the light danced on the wall. The light danced as he moved the mirror. With a flick of his wrist, the light flash reflected in her face.

"You're on stage," he shouted. "You're on stage, you're on stage."

She reeled and stepped back.

In a soft voice, he asked, "How do you like it?" And she began to weep.

Be-In in Central Park, Easter Sunday, March 26, 1967

(All photographs © 1990 by Fred W. McDarrah)

Outside the League for Spiritual Discovery's Ashram on
Hudson Street: Gregory Corso, Allen Ginsberg, William S.
Burroughs and Tibetan Goddess Maretta (Ericka Green),
February 15, 1967

Louis and Allen Ginsberg reading poetry and debating at the
Brooklyn Academy of Music, March 15, 1968

Ed Sanders in his Peace Eye Bookstore, 383 East 10th Street, January 14, 1966

Diggers Ritchie and Suzi, September 22, 1967

The Digger Free Store,
264 East 10th Street,
September 22, 1967

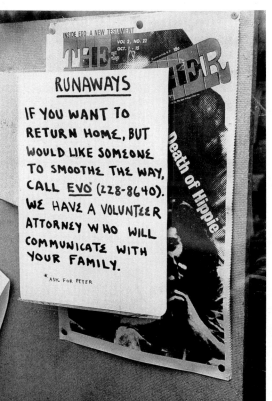

Sign on window of the
East Village Other's
storefront, Avenue B
and 9th Street,
November 12, 1967

The 3rd Street Sweep-In, April 8, 1967

Mayor John Lindsay tours Tompkins Square Park, Lower East Side August 21, 1967

Deputy Inspector Joseph Fink (center), Ninth Precinct,
May 24, 1968

The Group Image tribe in its East Village loft, April 26, 1968

Abbie and Anita Hoffman during chaos at the Yip-In at
Grand Central Station, March 22, 1968

BACK ON THE ROAD

HOW THE HAIGHT HAPPENED

Once upon a long time ago there was a kid at a Major American University who came to realize that fraternities were futile and grades were garbage and degrees were degrading. So he dropped out. He didn't drop into anything. He just dropped out. This kid was like no other kid. He was 4-F because he had six toes on his left foot, and he was proud of it, so he wore sandals. Now the one thing that this kid really grooved on was whistling in the fog. And one day he heard that no place had fog like San Francisco, so he went to San Francisco. When he arrived he discovered that not only did San Francisco have fog— really more than he needed—but it had a huge park that was out of sight for whistling. So he found a cheap apartment close to the park in a quiet neighborhood called Haight-Ashbury.

One foggy morning he was whistling around the park when he heard a hum. Another kid walked out of the fog. He was wearing sandals too. True, he had only five toes, but they had something in common.

"I heard your hum," our kid said. "It was nice."

"And you do a nice whistle," the other kid said. "I never could whistle."

"Nice fog, huh?" our kid said.

"It's not bad for humming," the other kid said. "Say, are you a head?" It was a long time ago.

"Ahead of what?"

"Never mind. Here," he said, giving our kid a sugar cube. "It'll help you whistle and it's fun."

It did and it was.

After a while a lot more kids had come to the quiet neighborhood by the park. Some of them liked fog and some of them liked music and some of them liked acid and most of them liked each other. One day someone thought that it would be groovy if they all got together all at once. So they did, one day in the park, and they called it a Be-In, and there were thousands and thousands of them, and it really felt good. It looked good too. It looked so good that *Life* did a photo spread on it, and it looked so good in *Life* that other magazines sent photographers and reporters to Haight-Ashbury.

"It's the beginning of a new age," our kid sighed, "but it's too crowded to whistle," and he left for Bodega Bay, where he heard there was even more fog.

THE GREAT SUMMER DROPOUT

June 1967—As twenty million kids cram for finals from Boston to Little Rock, San Francisco is quaking with anticipation. In years past, the "in" locations for summer vacations have been pretty far out. Katmandu last year. Marrakech the year before. This year it is indisputably the Haight, and anyone with a month's paper-route profits can make the pilgrimage.

Visions of a psychedelic *Grapes of Wrath,* half-fare caravans winging to hippie mecca, a quarter million kids going to be received at the Golden Gate ghetto.

It is all feasible, highly feasible, and Diggers and city officials tremble as one. The Diggers have come a long way since they first passed out stew in the Panhandle. They now have four farms growing free food for the Haight. The profits from the Monterey Pop Festival will go to the Diggers for more groceries. And, after Police Chief Cahill denied squatting rights in Golden Gate Park, the Diggers have been seeking out ghost towns and rural land for hippie Hoovervilles.

Two great gatherings are likely to indicate the scope of the summer invasion. The Los Angeles *Oracle* family, some twenty-eight people who turn out a newspaper from a turn-of-the-century mansion complete with badminton courts, have leased 160 acres six miles south of the Grand Canyon rim for a Gathering of the Tribes. The logistics of the land, a part of Kaibab National Forest, are intimidating. At seven thousand feet, the temperatures are extreme even in June. Celebrants must come prepared for rigorous camping, and all water must be carried in.

Furthermore, the Indians are upset about the Be-In. The Hopi have met the hippies before, but they are intimidated by the prospect of a mass invasion. San Francisco's Communication Company issued a report on a Hopi-Hippie conference on the Be-In late in April. Even the hippies were down on the gathering.

Larry Bird, who has lived with the Hopi for some time, warned about Arizona cops who, he said, "are already arresting 150 hitchhikers a week and slamming them into small-town jails forever."

Emmett Grogan, the Digger, questioned the motives of the gathering. "We are hungry for our own rituals and lines of life," he said. "But there is no need on behalf of the people to organize a Be-In. The people will develop their own rituals. They will build their courage and leave Be-Ins to the college students, ad-men, and news media. They will look to their brothers, not the men who claim to be their leaders."

So the Communication Company came out editorially against the Grand Canyon gathering, and is organizing a rival solstice celebration for June 21 in Golden Gate Park. A recent CC communiqué explained that "this will not be a passive Be-In (repetition is foolish) but an active celebration, a Do-In, if you wish, and many groups, tribes, and clans are planning events for all to share. CC is sponsoring pagan and otherwise magical ceremonies proper to the time, to be conducted by Dame Sybil Leek.

Also planned: six steers will be roasted whole. This is the first pagan Midsummer Festival since the fall of Rome, perhaps."

Haul out your Tibetan prayer wheel and spin a prayer for the Haight. The Great Summer Dropout of 1967 is about to begin.

FUNERAL NOTICE

HIPPIE

In the
Haight-Ashbury District
of this city,

Hippie, devoted son
of
Mass Media

Friends are invited
to attend services
beginning at sunrise,
October 6, 1967

at

Buena Vista Park

WHAT DIED IN SAN FRANCISCO?

The season changed, and the moon thrusts of the Autumn Equinox preoccupied the many people in

Haight-Ashbury who chart by planetary movement. Others participated in the Equinox celebration, a pleasant event which has become a tradition here in the past few seasons. This celebration was of special note, because two traditional American Indian medicine men decided at the last minute to attend. The medicine men, Rolling Thunder and Shaymu, came to the Straight Theater on Haight Street and helpers hurried to the street with handbills reading "QUICK INDIANS WANT TO SEE YOU." The natives came, and, in front of the Straight, Rolling Thunder met Shaymu, and Shaymu said, "Let us adopt these people, who are called hippies, as our children. They have been disowned." Rolling Thunder agreed, and the Indians and many of their new children went to the country to dance all night around a fire on a beach.

The vast majority of the younger residents of Haight-Ashbury just hung around the street, aware of neither the Equinox nor of their new family. Most were unaware because they didn't care. They had more pressing problems: to find some bread to get home, to find a place to crash for the night, or to find some speed so they could forget about the night. Haight Street was lined with people with problems. Behind the scenes, there were only more problems.

Most of the tourists were gone, and with them their funny money, which really didn't matter because they only clogged the streets and not much of the money filtered back into the community anyway. But the community was certainly short of bread. The Haight-Ashbury Medical Clinic, which had given free medical treatment to thirteen thousand people since June without any financial or moral support from government or foundation sources, finally closed its doors, defeated and depleted, on

September 22. The Digger Free Store was in debt and the proprietor threatened to split to New York unless the $750.00 in back rent materialized. The Switchboard, which maintained a volunteer legal staff of thirty lawyers and had found crash pads for up to three hundred pilgrims a night, was doing fine until it received some contributions. They spent the money before the checks bounced, and needed $1,000.00 to survive. Most of the communes in the country still depended on outside support, and even the free food in the Panhandle, which began to resemble a bread line, threatened to fold without more funds.

Haight-Ashbury had survived the Summer of Love, but it seemed mortally wounded.

It could have been worse. Estimates in the spring had doubled the estimated fifty thousand saints and freeloaders who came to the Haight seeking the love and free life that the papers had promised. The subdivided flats in the bay-windowed houses—the rule in Haight-Ashbury as tenement apartments are on the Lower East Side—stretched to accommodate guests. There were no hunger riots, and the now-defunct free medical clinic kept the threatened plague and pestilence in check. The pilgrims were fed and housed—with occasional free music and drugs thrown in—and the panhandlers on Haight Street were still asking for quarters in October.

As I arrived, there were kids on many corners with packs on their backs and thumbs stuck out trying to leave. The people I met, many of whom had been here before the Human Be-In and the Summer of Love (some of whom had coined the words), were exhausted and dejected, rather like a bartender counting unbroken glasses after an all-night brawl. Yet they were counting broken

spirits and their few veteran friends who had not yet split
for the sanctum of an unpublicized commune in the country. They were the hosts of the Summer of Love and now,
after the Autumn Equinox, it was time to clean up.

There's not much reason now to go to Haight Street
unless it's to cop. The street itself has a layer of grease and
dirt which is common on busy sidewalks in New York but
rare in San Francisco, a film that comes from bits of lunch,
garbage, and spilled Coke ground into the cement by the
heels of Haight Street strollers. It is not a pleasant place
to sit, yet hundreds do, huddled in doorways or stretched
out on the sidewalk, in torn blankets and bare feet, bored
voices begging for spare change, selling two-bit psychedelic newspapers that were current in the spring, and
dealing, dealing, dealing. The dealing is my strongest impression of Haight Street. The housewives with their
Brownie cameras miss the best part of the show.

It's not hard to cop in the Haight. If you look remotely
hip and walk down the street, a dozen anxious peddlers
should approach you to offer their goods. It is something
that may happen once a day on St. Mark's Place. Here I
am asked several times on each block whether I want to
buy, or occasionally sell, grass, acid, meth, kilos, lids,
matchboxes or, in the case of one ambitious (and, I think,
mad) merchant, "Owsley tabs, mescaline, psilocybin-
coated grass, or anything, anything you want." The merchant was young, fat, owlish-looking, perspiring, and un-
shaven. He had an entourage of several preadolescent
kids swathed in Army blankets. "I know the stuff is good,"
he said. "I try it all myself."

The pace of dealing picks up at night, when the dark
provides some protection. Walking down Haight Street at

night, the offers are whispers in the shadows or in the crowds. Mostly it's acid. But street acid is usually a combination of a taste of acid fortified with anything from methedrine to strychnine. There have been a lot of bad trips here lately, because there has been a lot of bad acid.

Even in October some new stores are opening, latecomers for the leftovers of the poster and bead market, but it should be a rough winter for the bead game, with no assurance that next summer the circus will come to town again. Enlightened natives have spread out all over town from Haight-Ashbury. Anyone curious about hippies can pick up a hitchhiker or find some on his own block. Unlike Greenwich Village, the shops are not an attraction in themselves. The same goods are sold in more attractive shops all over town.

I did find one merchant who wanted nothing to do with the psychedelic market. I needed some matches so I went into a liquor store on Haight Street off Clayton and, rather than hassle the thin, white-haired man at the counter, I bought a pack of cigarettes, which he gave me with a pack of matches. Then I asked for an extra pack of matches.

He eyed me severely.

"You got matches, right here," he said, tapping the pack of matches with the nail of his index finger.

"I'd like an extra pack," I said. "I'll pay you for them."

He shook his head. "No," he said, "you got matches right here. One pack is all you need. One pack of cigarettes. One pack of matches. What do you need more for?"

I pulled out my other pack of cigarettes. "For these," I said. "That's what I came here for."

"What happened to the matches you got with those?"

he shouted, triumphant with the evidence, finding me guilty of all the dope-fiend–marijuana-puffing sins that the mind of a liquor store keeper could imagine. Even after the hordes, he was holding his hill. He was doing his bit.

The street is the heart of the Haight. It is where everyone first realized that they had company on their trip. It is reality—a hard fact to stomach when you're fifteen and strung out on meth and it's midnight and you've got no place to crash except a doorway. Without the coffeehouses and bars of the beats, the street is the scene, a hell of a scene, with tourists and runaways and dealers and burners and the holy Angels with their bikes and the gaudy stores as a backdrop.

A schism exists between the street and the elite in Haight-Ashbury. The same is true in New York. The elite of the Haight-Ashbury scene are more aware of it, and they have occasionally tried to bridge the gap, without much success. Chester Anderson began the Communication Company over a year ago, hoping to keep the street in touch and control with an "instant newspaper" of enticing handbills. The handbills fascinated the fringes but bored the masses. Anderson was finally purged and split several months ago for Florida. The Diggers tried harder, attacking the needs of the neighborhood with free food and free stores and free theater and free thought. They convinced Jay and Ron Thelin, pioneer proprietors of the Psychedelic Shop, to forsake free enterprise and just be free. The shop became a lounge for the street and finally died October 6 with the proprietors in debt, in love, and enlightened. On that day, the elders decided to put an end to it all.

The idea was kindled at a meeting earlier in the week at Happening House, a beautiful Victorian mansion just off the Panhandle on Clayton Street, which opened at the end of the summer to serve as a community center. The idea was to have a three-day funeral for the death of hip —or the death of the Haight—and most of the meeting was spent trying to determine just what had died. But all agreed that a funeral was a good idea. "The idea of a few people going down Haight Street," sighed *Oracle* editor Allen Cohen. "The idea, the symbol goes through walls, through windows, through air, through mountains. Through the media, it will hit millions of people." The media giveth and the media taketh away.

"I'm going to be driving the truck all day," a Digger said, "and I'm going to be talking to people."

"What are you going to tell them to do?" someone asked.

"I'm gonna tell them that everything's out of control. That they're free."

And then someone read the surrender speech of Chief Joseph of the Nez Perce and the meeting was adjourned.

After the meeting I walked with several of the talkers to the house of the Grateful Dead, where Rolling Thunder, the Shoshone medicine man, was staying while he visited Haight-Ashbury. It is a four-story Victorian townhouse, glowing with stained-glass windows, which clings to the hill on Ashbury Street and houses the Dead, their entourage, and the offices of the Haight-Ashbury Legal Organization. Rolling Thunder was sitting in the parlor.

Had it not been for his turquoise headband and heavy necklaces, which he said were given to him since he arrived in Haight-Ashbury, Rolling Thunder would hardly have looked like an Indian, let alone a medicine man. His skin is light and his face bears the hard lines of the harsh weather in the country of the Western Shoshone, which is Eastern Nevada. His hair is short and combed back and he wore the simple clothes of a rancher. He is soft-spoken, with a slight Western drawl, and loves to talk, making him the most candid prophet one could ever hope to meet.

Rolling Thunder, who is chairman of the traditional Tribal Council of the Western Shoshone Nation, came to San Francisco to join thirty-two traditional Indians who were about to embark on a caravan to circle the country to protest a bill pending in Congress which will allow Indians to borrow money on their lands. He believes that the bill is a trick to deprive the Indians of their remaining lands.

But the real threat of the bill before Congress, Rolling Thunder explained, is that it endangers the lands of the Hopi, which have always remained intact. "The Hopi are the keepers of our religion," he said. "As soon as we found out that the white man was taking everything, our sacred tablets were hidden with the Hopi.

"I was praying for my people," he recalled, "and I had a dream. I was in a kiva. I saw a fire—blue and green—in the dark at the far side. I knew it was a presence. I know it was the Supreme Being. He was covered with eagle feathers. He had a beak like an eagle and a body like a man. He said to look to the left. I looked and saw stone tablets with pictographs. He said, look there and you'll find an answer.

"A few days later I was in Hopi land, and they brought out the stone tablets, and I read them.

"They said, in the last days the Hopi would be the last

to go. That's happening now, so we know the time is close."

The caravan is intended to fulfill the prophecy which speaks of two stars in the sky. "For hundreds of years," Rolling Thunder said, "the large star followed the small star across the sky. And the Great Spirit said, when the stars reverse, the time is right. That happened two months ago. He also said that we should go out and meet people, to see who is true and who is not true. And that is what we are doing."

The prophecy also speaks of destruction, that after the stars reverse a "gourd of ashes" will fall from the sky, destroying the people who are not true. "It's written on the rocks," Rolling Thunder said, "and when that comes people will come to the wilderness to seek refuge with the Indians and they'll try to buy their way in, but their money will be of no value. We will know who is true and who is not true."

Thelin explained the idea of the funeral. "We're really trying to sabotage the word 'hippie,'" he said. "It's really fucking us up. It's not our word. It has nothing to do with us. We'd like to substitute 'free American' in its place."

Rolling Thunder smiled and nodded. "That 'free American' term sounds a lot better," he said. "I've asked several people what they call themselves, and they couldn't give me an answer. Now maybe they can give me an answer."

The medicine man sat on a large desk, and a dozen people sat around him on the floor. "I saw this before it ever happened," he said. "This is a direct prophecy from myself. I wondered if the white man could ever live in this country and eat the food and still remain a hashed-over European. And I saw these people with the long hair. These people will be the future Americans.

"What you people are going through is the same thing that we've gone through. You're just getting your training. We'll help you in any way we can.

"There will also be people among you who will be medicine men. He will know protection. He will know what areas are safe. There's one among you already. He doesn't know it. I've talked to him and he will be coming to my country to learn. But, until you have your own, you can borrow one once in a while.

"It's going to be rough," he warned. "It's going to be violent, especially in the cities. The Spirit told me to stay away from that violence. I think that might be good advice for you people. Violence is not the way. There's something more powerful than that.

"In the last days, they will throw everything at you to destroy you, and that's what's happening now. And now the medicine men are coming back. When those stars reversed—that is when the power of good took over from the power of evil. Many young people are becoming medicine men. So now your people, who are living like Indians, you see what you've let yourselves into.

"They may prosecute and jail people. They may do everything, because they are fearful. But they won't succeed."

Someone asked about the Shoshone way of facing death.

"Death?" the medicine man asked. "There is no death. But if you kill yourself, you displease the Great Spirit, and you may be reincarnated as a worm."

Rolling Thunder's daughter, who was with him, said that she was walking down to Haight Street, and asked if there was anything she could do for him.

"I'll tell you one thing you can do," he said. "You can go

down to the Psychedelic Shop and get some of those 'We Shall Overcome' buttons. Those will be very popular up in our country. Can we get them wholesale?"

"They might for you," someone said. "They should know you."

"Then I guess I'd better walk down myself."

The next day was a day of preparation and press conferences. I walked into the Psychedelic Shop in the late afternoon to find CBS News waiting in line behind a local television station to interview Ron Thelin in his tiny office at the back of the shop. A tiny enameled American flag hung from Thelin's freshly pierced ear.

The funeral notices had been printed. They were small, stiff cards, bordered in black, reading "HIPPIE. In the Haight-Ashbury district of this city, Hippie, devoted son of Mass Media. Friends are invited to attend services beginning at sunrise, October 6, 1967, at Buena Vista Park."

And there was a handbill, which read in part:

MEDIA CREATED THE HIPPIE WITH YOUR HUNGRY CONSENT. BE SOMEBODY. CAREERS ARE TO BE HAD FOR THE ENTERPRISING HIPPIE. DEATH OF HIPPIE END. FINISHED HIPPYEE GONE GOODBYE HEHPPEEE DEATH DEATH HHIPPEE. EXORCISE HAIGHT-ASHBURY. CIRCLE THE ASHBURY. FREE THE BOUNDARIES. OPEN EXORCISE. YOU ARE FREE. WE ARE FREE. DO NOT BE RECREATED. BE-LIEVE ONLY IN YOUR OWN INCARNATE SPIRIT. BIRTH OF FREE MAN. FREE SAN FRANCISCO. INDEPENDENCE. FREE AMERICANS. BIRTH. DO NOT BE BOUGHT WITH A PICTURE, A PHRASE. DO NOT BE CAPTURED IN WORDS. THE CITY IS OURS. YOU ARE ARE ARE. TAKE WHAT IS YOURS. THE BOUNDARIES ARE DOWN. SAN FRANCISCO IS FREE NOW FREE THE TRUTH IS OUT OUT OUT.

And, at the bottom, according to the prophecy of October 6, 1966, the day the California LSD laws came into effect, the Declaration of Independence was redeclared.

Saturday morning the little windows in the parking meters up and down Haight Street were all painted white, and the faithful gathered before dawn at the top of the hill in Buena Vista Park to greet the sun. The sun rose on time, and they rang bells and breathed deeply and exhaled "Om," the first sound in the Universe. Then the pallbearers lifted the fifteen-foot coffin, to be filled with the artifacts of hip, and bore it down the long hill to the street. They paused to kneel at the crossroads of Haight and Ashbury and brought the coffin to rest for the moment in front of the Psychedelic Shop, which had a huge sign reading "Be Free" in place of its famous mandala. Then the elated mourners swept the street, in preparation for the procession at noon.

At noon a huge banner was stretched across the street. It read "Death of Hippie, Freebie, Birth of the Free Man." (The *Chronicle* had dubbed the reincarnated hippie a "freebie" in a story on Friday, but later apologized.) The coffin was carried to the Panhandle, where more newspapers, beads, fruit, cookies, posters, flowers, and buttons were added to the remains. A banner was held up reading "The Brotherhood of Free Men Is Born." And, as the procession began, the crowd sang "Hare Krishna," but slowly, as a dirge.

The procession moved slowly down the Panhandle toward Golden Gate Park. First came a legion of photographers, walking backwards, and then the coffin, over ten struggling pallbearers, and then a hippie laid out on a stretcher, holding a flower to his chest, and then about two hundred mourners, some in elaborate costume, some shaking tambourines, some carrying babies, some dodging cameras. When it reached the park the procession turned left, now with a police escort, whose job seemed to be to keep the procession jammed onto the sidewalk. Six blocks later they turned left again, hauling the coffin up the steep hill on Frederick Street, and at the top of the hill, they turned again on Masonic Street, which goes steeply downhill, to complete the circle of the Haight. The coffin picked up speed as it moved downhill, the photographers jumped to get out of the way, and the dead hippie squirmed to stay on the stretcher. And then, halfway down the steep Masonic Street sidewalk, their path was blocked.

A Cadillac had been left parked in a driveway.

The funeral procession came to a crushing halt, and the police escort—a lone cop—sauntered over and began to write out a parking ticket.

"Move the car," someone yelled. The owner walked out of the house and began to argue with the cop.

"Hassle him later," they yelled. "Move the car!"

The cop gave the man a ticket, and the owner returned to his house. The Cadillac remained in the driveway, and the pallbearers were groaning.

At which point the cop consented to let the procession bypass the car in the street.

The procession ended where it began, in the Panhandle. The hippie on the stretcher rose from the dead, looking punchy, and the banners were used to kindle a fire under the huge coffin. The flames took to it quickly and rose ten feet in the air as the crowd cheered. They danced in a circle around the burning coffin and the cameramen and, as the charred coffin crumbled and the fire died down, free men began to leap over the flames. Then the crowd gasped with horror as they saw the fire engines approach.

"The remains!" someone yelled. "Don't let them put it out!" The crowd blocked the firemen and spokesmen argued with the chief as his men readied their hoses. When the hoses were ready, the crowd parted, and the coffin disappeared in a monster cloud of spray and black smoke. The fire was out in seconds, and the firemen moved in with shovels to break apart the smouldering remains. A few diehards were still arguing with the chief, but the mourners had already begun to wander off.

Saturday, the *Chronicle* reverently reported that the Hippie was dead, but by Monday they were back in business again, with their daily quota of copy from the Haight. The banner remained strung across Haight Street for a week, as a reminder, and the Psychedelic Shop was closed and boarded up, and the parking meters were cleaned of the white paint. But the kids still panhandled and sold newspapers and lounged in the doorways, and the occasional tourist still gawked from behind the locked doors of his car. Nothing had changed. It was all the same.

But an exorcism is a subtle thing, and some of the dejection that plagued the Haight in the wake of the Summer of Love did appear to be gone. When a phalanx of fourteen cops swept down Haight Street Tuesday in a daylight raid to net runaways, the community responded with vigor and outrage and, despite threats by Police Chief Cahill, the raids were not repeated. The heat was on and the Haight kept cool.

Within a few weeks, the Switchboard was out of debt and danger, and a series of well-attended benefits brought a generous reserve of funds into the coffers of the

clinic, which reopened in late October. The Straight Theatre, which was denied a dance permit by an ever-harass-
ing city, held huge "Dance Classes" (for which permits
are not needed) to the accompaniment of the Grateful
Dead. And the Diggers were delivering free meat to communes and distributing 5,000 copies of a twenty-page free
magazine called *Free City*.

The elders now harbor hopes that San Francisco will
indeed become a "free city." If any city can, it can, but it
must be born, not made. The hippie was made but the
community called Haight-Ashbury was born, and it was a
virgin birth—an evolutionary experiment and experience.
It was beautiful, I am told, in the golden age before the
Human Be-In which awoke the media to the precious
copy lying untapped on the south side of Golden Gate
Park. "Were you here a year ago?" people ask. If you
were, then you know.

But then the seekers came en masse, enticed by the
media. "They came to the Haight," a handbill relates,
"with a great need and a great hunger for a loving community. Many, wanting to belong, identified with the
superficial aspects of what 'hippie' was. They didn't drop
out but rather changed roles.

"As a result the tone of Haight-Ashbury changed. With
many people coming in expecting to be fed and housed,
the older community tried to fulfill their needs. Rather
than asking them to do their thing, the community tried
to give them what they came for. The community tried to
be something it wasn't.

"The early members tried to save the community and as
a result it began to die. It began to die because in the
effort to save it, the individuals lost themselves. Without
individual selves the community started to become a shell

with little within; to maintain the community feeling, meetings replaced relationships and organization replaced community.

"By the end of the summer we were forming organizations to save something that no longer existed. Community is a creative thing and saving is only a holding action. By desperate clinging, we lost."

They lost, but they learned.

THE RUNAWAYS

Larry Kemp almost became a folk hero in the East Bay area. For several weeks in early October, his distraught mother ran huge display ads in the *Berkeley Barb* headlined "LARRY KEMP COME HOME" over a picture of a smiling fourteen-year-old kid with hair down to his eyes and creeping over his ears. In the back pages of the *Barb*, Mrs. Kemp ran additional spot ads, with just the headline in large, black type. And relatives and friends sprinkled appeals through the classifieds, saying "Larry, call us if you want to talk." Finally Larry got the message. The *Barb* ran a follow-up story saying that Larry and his mother—after an absence of three weeks—were reunited. Both refused comment.

It is possible that Larry had run off to enlist in the Marines and that his mother, who might have been a diehard pacifist, was in grief over her son's defection. It is far more likely that Larry was one of the thousands of youths who fled to live free in the environs of Haight-Ashbury. The pilgrimage peaked in the summer and by October most of the runaways, like Larry Kemp, had reconciled and returned home.

The kids who remained on the doorsteps and stoops of Haight Street had come for more than a vacation. Those among them who were runaways were now also truant. The kids who remained in October obviously did not intend to return to school. The kids who had not yet been apprehended were less likely to have come from families of influence. They were the leftovers of the Summer of Love.

On October 9, San Francisco Police Chief Thomas Cahill decided that the underage youths remaining in Haight-Ashbury were finally fair game. He ordered a daylight raid of Haight Street to net runaways. Fourteen policemen walking in a phalanx on the sidewalks picked up thirty-two youths in a matter of minutes and took them to the Park Street Station where eleven of them, proving their age, were immediately released. The others were turned over to juvenile authorities.

Cahill was criticized for the raid, but he defended his decision. "I don't have to make excuses to anybody," he declared. "If those who were criticizing had children who were swallowed up in that jungle, they'd have a different story." Cahill reportedly is unable to conceive of an ungrateful parent. Most of the parents, in fact, solidly backed his use of force.

It is a time when force appears to many to be the only solution to incomprehensible problems. In a time of infectious war and domestic insurgency, America is losing its youth to a mysterious, invisible, and invincible Pied Piper. The American white middle class is in the realm of last resorts.

The runaways, however, would contend that the mystery is not where they're running to. Haight-Ashbury is the most overexposed neighborhood in the country. The mystery, they say, is at the source. The middle-class home is a curious thing, a wall-to-wall womb of impersonal affluence and controlled climate regulated by the barometric pressures of status, media, and an uncompromising fear of anything that is unfamiliar. "What is the straight world?" a young girl asked. "They think we're funny. I wonder if they ever stop to think how strange they are."

There has never been a generation so detached from their parents. All of the practical binds are gone. It has been decades since the average middle-class family needed their adolescent children for anything more than dish-washing, baby-sitting, and lawn-mowing. For the parents, the postwar ties were emotional ones; for the children, the ties were material. Now the children, by rejecting the parents' material values, also throw off the need of support. The society has reached such a point of affluence that a resourceful kid can live off its waste. A kid who lacks resources can live off his peers, who are, more often than not, willing to sustain him. Every commune carries a few.

The detachment is furthered by the notorious alienation that plagues the adolescent in the Great Society. One of the more popular expressions of this alienation has been the use of psychedelic drugs, which offer detachment inconceivable to the outsider. A fourteen-year-old girl on a bad trip doesn't call for her mother because her mother wouldn't know what to do. Sometimes she wishes she could. For all the publicized camaraderie, hers is often a lonely quest.

It is a common feeling among drug users that there is an unbreachable communications gap between them and those people who have not turned on. Many of the ethics and mores of the hippie movement have as their source the psychedelic experience. Many still revere acid as an oracle. But there is the will to communicate, if not the means. A lot of kids talk about turning-on their parents. Hash fruit cakes will be big this Christmas.

And the detachment is reinforced by the life they must lead. Many of the kids are going through hell. They see what their parents never dreamed possible. They are going through a space-age rite of purification, which usually begins with de-purification. Many are infected by guilt, which is only partly offset by a dogged pride and determination that drives them through the streets and the crash pads and the amphetamine vigils. "I'd like to make it my own way," a runaway said. "I won't go home until I prove something to myself."

Many runaways feel betrayed by their parents, a conviction that is reinforced when they are pursued. But they know that they have the future in their own hands. Some have already considered alternative methods of raising children. I met a girl from New York who had dropped out of high school the previous week. She was reading *Summerhill,* and digging it. Others are joining in living community experiments—which may psychologically serve as substitute families—where members support and take care of each other. Some of these, like New York's Group Image, have been successful. Others, like Lou Gottlieb's Morning Star Ranch, have been disastrous.

Few parents have the patience of the father of Mouse,

famed San Francisco poster artist, who wrote to *Ramparts* magazine from his home in Michigan saying with obvious pride that his long-haired son Stanley (Mouse), whose portrait appeared on the cover of *Ramparts*'s hippie issue, resembled his mother.

The more typical parent, his fears inflamed with the sensational coverage of the brutal double slaying of Linda Hutchinson and Groovy in New York, would probably see the adolescent underground in a *Lord of the Flies* horror vision of a world of children gone mad. He would see another front of anarchy. He might see something he clearly does not understand, something obviously alien but intuitively personal to him among the hippies, and he would probably feel threatened by it. A sexually frustrated society feels threatened by long hair and free love among its youth. Its own children seem strangers.

"I'll tell you why your children look so strange," Gregory Corso yelled at the mothers of America last spring. "They're not your children. They've been reborn."

It has now been reasonably demonstrated that the famous "hippie" was a fabrication of the mass media. The media did it unconsciously, but it happened nonetheless. Many individuals who were trapped by the label adapted to it, and the essence of their individuality was lost. Once contained and packaged, they began to be oppressed, as the public reacted to the symbols it could see through the goldfish bowl of the media. Hippies, the public observed, were weird, immoral, dirty, misguided, disloyal, unproductive, and they used dope. The Establishment sought refuge in weak jokes. Governor Ronald Reagan defines a hippie as someone who "dresses like Tarzan, has hair like Jane, and smells like Cheetah."

Now that the attention of the media has been captured

by the under-age refugees from affluence, the term "runaway" is also becoming an arbitrary label and a stigma. Like "hippie" it brings instant images to mind: innocence, virginity, murder, rape, and even "hippies," who are, in turn, weird, immoral, dirty, misguided, and so forth. Finally the deserted parents—and parents have been deserted for years—have a symbol to which they can anxiously cling. Many react predictably, like Mr. and Mrs. Charles A. Schoeneck, Jr., who mercilessly pursued their fleeing daughter, terrified that someone might get in before she comes out.

Senator Abraham Ribicoff responded to the inviting opportunity to bolster motherhood by introducing a bill which would bring the FBI into the search for runaway juveniles and missing persons. The bill provided for a computerized system of tracking and identification.

For although "runaway" has become a label like "hippie," it reflects a legal reality. The runaway seldom faces arrest, but he may be legally detained at any time. As a minor, he lacks many privileges of due process which have saved his elders in countless pot busts. His case is seldom dismissed for lack of evidence or illegal search and seizure. He is a ward of his parents in another world.

His status threatens him even in his own world. The runaway is a fugitive and he may bring on the heat. He may be ostracized because of this. He must dodge cops and find false ID. He may—with good reason—be afraid to go out on the street. He may feel like a Vietcong.

I was talking with a fifteen-year-old kid with false ID and a blanket. "I've been here three days," he said. "Do you think I'll last a month?"

· · ·

The Tuesday after the runaway net was hurled over Haight Street, some of the community elders met the press. It was intended to be a rare meeting between community spokesmen and representatives from Police Chief Cahill's office, but when the cops saw the press cars parked in front of Happening House, where the meeting was held, they split. The elders salvaged the morning by bitching to the media.

Their main complaint was that while they needed protection from the police, they only received harassment. In the middle of the police raid on Haight Street, they charged, a clothing store three blocks away was robbed of $700.00 worth of suede jackets. They accurately pointed out that Haight Street, once a small business street of a quiet neighborhood next to Golden Gate Park, is now the frequent scene of intimidation and robbery. They denied, however, that the neighborhood was the primary source of narcotics on the West Coast and they said that, contrary to Cahill's allegations, motorcycle gangs were not trying to take over Haight-Ashbury. "There's nothing left to take over," one explained.

The press gave the conference generous coverage, but the next day a small group of people who are working together in a stoned communications experiment under the code name of agit-free, decided that the message should be made more emphatic. They decided to hold an emergency conference on runaways, that is, a "Runaway Emergency Conference," which would bring "Clergy, police, juvenile authorities, young people, parents, professionals, and certain elements of the free community" together in a panel discussion. Huckleberry's, a housing and referral service for runaways, and Happening House, which opened in September to serve as a community center, would sponsor the symposium, which was to be held at the Straight Theatre. What their handbill didn't say—it only hinted—was that agit-free had planned a surprise.

The panel was as surprised as the audience when the lights in the theater began to flash menacingly and runaways, wearing black hoods, came in to testify and some loud-mouth puppets joined the panel, and voices began to come out of the wall. The voices were young, taped in the street, and they spoke in revealing clichés. Their words were punctuated by the sounds of surf, heartbeats, and a baby crying.

"He didn't know any other way to reach me . . . She can't understand it . . . You learn so much about people in two days. It's really unbelievable . . . There's respect for me as an individual that was never there before because I went out and did my thing . . . My father punished me twice by shaving my head . . . You know, now they're willing to listen but they don't know what's going on . . . I think the only freedom is death."

And while the panelists talked to the puppets and the voices spoke from the walls, "instant newspaper" handbills were distributed in the audience. Some were about wildlife: "On leaving home, the young woodrat either takes up residence in a nearby abandoned home erected by another woodrat or starts building one of its own." Another read: "You are the information." There were a dozen more.

The climax of the symposium was a series of nude dances, accompanied by a rock group. Six members of the Jane Lapiner dance group—three men and three women—danced completely nude before the audience of five hundred. (The dances had been performed at the

Straight Theatre for several weeks.) Suddenly someone shouted that the police were entering. The audience rose as one and rushed to the dance floor to cover the dancers while they dressed. The police were foiled.

But not entirely. Dr. Leonard Wolf, forty-four, a San Francisco State College professor and director of Happening House, allegedly approached the police and claimed responsibility for the event. Police charged him with contributing to the delinquency of minors.

A few days later I walked up to Huckleberry's, a tall, brown Victorian house at 1 Broderick Street on the south side of Buena Vista Park. The people at Huckleberry's have become specialists on runaways, if there is such a thing. Their success has intrigued professionals concerned with the runaway problem in the Bay Area, and the backbone of the organization is an active group of more than thirty professional volunteers.

In early June, several elders in the Haight-Ashbury community requested help in the runaway problem. They had tried to work with the runaways themselves, but ran into legal and financial problems. The Glide Foundation, an angel to many Haight-Ashbury activities, heard the appeal and, with the help of the Regional Young Adult Project and the San Francisco Council of Churches, worked through the San Francisco Foundation to set up Huckleberry's.

Huckleberry's was envisioned as a neutral ground for runaways. "This is a place where you can go home without being defeated, where you can go home with a new contract," explained the Reverend Larry Beggs, thirty-four, a minister in the United Church of Christ who, with Barbara Brachman, twenty-five, a social worker, directs Huckleberry's. "We feel that everyone in the family bears responsibility for conflict. We feel that it's a waste of time just to move bodies back to home without getting at root problems. Society is lazy. It delegates the policeman into what is a family problem. We feel that this just perpetuates culprit mentality and resentment. All present methods are on the police type of thing where they just move bodies around. Our long goal is to relieve the police force of a job they're not trained to do."

When a runaway arrives at Huckleberry's, he is met by Beggs or Brachman, and interviewed by an intake volunteer. If he decides to stay at the house, his parents are contacted and asked to sign legal waivers. "We discuss the family situation briefly," Beggs explained, "and give referrals to family therapists, whose bias is not to talk about sickness, but communication. I ask the parents to come in to get their kids and to see the area. They've come from Yakima, Seattle, Utah. Then a meeting is arranged. We have long sessions here, one to four hours in length. Sometimes they get pretty wild."

From June 18 to October 20, 274 youths were interviewed at Huckleberry's—180 male and 94 female. Of the 274, 168 chose to contact their families; 128 of these returned voluntarily. Thirty more were returned by authorities, and the rest split.

"When the police come, we turn over the body," Beggs said. "There is no escape, no hiding. There were five incidents when parents used this place to trap their kids. We feel in that case that he's one up on them morally if not legally. But most parents go for this service instead of the police, and police have sent parents here." Over the past summer, 359 parents have called or come into Huckleberry's.

Half of the 274 youths who came to Huckleberry's were

from the Bay area. Half were from families that were not intact. Most of the kids who came to the house had been in Haight-Ashbury less than a week. "Most of the kids who come here are not making it or don't choose to make it," Beggs observed. "Most of them come in trusting right to the hilt. I think it's a place where they think we're pretty much for them."

If a runaway is interviewed and does not choose to contact his parents, he may not stay at Huckleberry's, but he does not go away empty-handed. He may consult with the professional staff and is given referral to free legal and medical aid. If, when the parents are contacted, they refuse the services of Huckleberry's or disclaim responsibility for the runaway, legal counsel is suggested to them regarding their responsibility and they are asked to pick up their kid. "If he has an extra-legal hang-up," Beggs said, "he may decide to turn himself in to the police." Of the 274, twenty have turned themselves in.

"We're abiding by the legal rules of how to play today's games," Beggs said, "but we're trying to reform those laws and change them. It's a risky game."

Beggs is a stanch proponent of juvenile rights. "A German shepherd has more rights than a kid," he said. "He can't be beaten. His sexual relations can't be restrained. Kids are restrained by the draft, compulsory education, sexual rights, reading rights, traveling rights, in the juvenile courts. And all those areas are being assailed by the juveniles themselves. This is a dot on the ocean of a whole surge in this country for self-determination for youth. It's a dramatic challenge to the colonial powers of the adult world.

"The key here is self-determination," he said. "We honor the decision-making process."

The story of Huckleberry's success has spread, and Beggs has answered inquiries from New York, Seattle, Dallas, Berkeley, and Portland asking for help and information about setting up similar houses.

Thus many people were surprised when, on October 20 (two days after the agit-free symposium) San Francisco police juvenile officers raided Huckleberry's, taking nine runaway guests to the Youth Guidance Center, where they were held on charges of having no parental supervision, and arrested Burjhild Oberhammer, twenty-four, the house manager. Then—at midnight—the police went to the Haight Street home of co-director Barbara Brachman, and picked her up. Beggs, who lives in Marin County, surrendered himself the next day to a warrant. All were charged with contributing to the delinquency of minors.

The police alleged that the action came from the complaint of the mother of a thirteen-year-old boy, who said her son had stayed there three days without permission. But the boy was not there when the police raided, and the police arrest report showed that all but one of the juveniles arrested told police that they had permission from their parents to stay at Huckleberry's.

"As well as we can determine, there were no grounds for the arrest," said the Reverend Ted McIlvenna, Methodist minister and general administrator of the house, at a press conference the next day. "We can only suspect this was a monumental mistake or that someone in our city is playing politics."

A major difference between the Haight-Ashbury and the East Village has been the relationship of the communities with their respective city governments. It is likely that a major factor has been the condition of the neighborhoods. The kids who moved into the Lower East Side brought new business and higher rents. They were peaceful in a violent neighborhood, relatively affluent in an impoverished neighborhood, a reality which the mayor's office and the precinct police carefully but gratefully recognize. It is the sort of relationship where streets may be closed for dances and parades, where Diggers can have emergency conferences with representatives of the mayor, where, indeed, there were four successive weeks of marijuana Smoke-Ins in Tompkins Square Park.

Haight-Ashbury, on the other hand, never had it so bad. It was a quiet, middle-class neighborhood of pleasant Victorian houses inhabited by quiet, middle-class people, and a few artists who liked to live close to Golden Gate Park. The Victorian houses, however, easily subdivided into flats, which easily stretched to accommodate guests, and since the stampede began the crime rate in the area has soared. The hell in Haight-Ashbury was of its own making, and it became a political issue. The city administration responded with unrelenting harassment of the Haight-Ashbury community.

The raid on Huckleberry's came a few weeks before a hotly contested mayoralty race went to the polls. The departing city administration favored Joseph Alioto, a law-and-order man, as a successor. The runaway issue was rich, and Alioto won.

Most of the runaways in Haight-Ashbury had probably never heard of Huckleberry's, or simply had no need for the services. Not all runaways flounder in their flight. Some are making it, and would decline to go home with a new contract or not. Some will remain through the winter, or may move south to escape the rains.

Beggs would agree, and he cautioned against dismissing runaways as a summer problem. "It's a brainwashed idea," he said. "Family problems are not seasonal. If anything, they're worse when school starts."

The bulletin board at the Switchboard in late October confirmed this. Actually the bulletin board had long since been overwhelmed by the snapshots and portraits and handbills and letters that covered most of the wall in the front room of the Switchboard offices. They were pathetic, impassioned appeals from deserted families.

The Switchboard began as a communications center, actually a telephone, which founder Al Rinker, thirty, installed to determine the needs of the Haight-Ashbury community. Soon the Switchboard began a free legal service, now working with thirty volunteer lawyers, and, through the long Summer of Love, the group found crash pads for anyone who walked through the door. The Switchboard dealt with staggering numbers: eighteen thousand kids came through the door over the summer, and four to five hundred runaways were reported, of whom one hundred got in touch with their parents.

The Switchboard lacks the program facilities of Huckleberry's. "Runaways we do not find," Rinker explained. "When the parents call, we put their names in the *Berkeley Barb*. If a kid calls and doesn't want to get in touch with his parents, we don't even tell the parents that kid called. We tell them that we cannot connect them."

The Switchboard has discontinued its crash-pad service in favor of apartment referral, but the legal services will continue. When I visited the house, late in October, it still had a feeling like London after the blitz.

Certainly the majority of the summer refugees had decided to return home.

It is not such a defeat as it might appear. Haight-

Ashbury was no Eden by the middle of June. It was a rough scene for a kid from the suburbs. It was a sudden and harsh initiation into a strange underworld of lovers and burners, of sensation and violence, lined with acid and laced with speed. It must have failed to live up to their expectations. "There was nothing bigger than they were," a Haight-Ashbury veteran said. "They had only their own trips."

The climate has changed throughout the country since the hippies emerged. The movement has stretched the muscles of the middle class. Maharishi Mahesh Yogi recruited disciples not only among the predisposed, but among account executives and fraternity presidents. Many of the kids who returned home did so under new contract. They may be turning on with their parents.

The return of the runaways may be an unconscious response to the evolutionary necessity of decentralization. The Haight-Ashbury is simply not necessary. It's become a drag. The kids returned to different regions, many determined to dig the country, and change it if they could. Hip movements are happening in many smaller communities, which has never happened before. The kids returned to the schools, and will be making radical demands for changes in the educational process, to which the schools must respond, for these are the students who are giving the Establishment a second chance.

Return is not surrender. The kids tasted freedom, utter independence, and pot, three tantalizing commodities that are hard to forget. They abandoned nothing by returning. Many are content to postpone their idyll for a while. Most have two or three years before they are threatened by the draft, and a lot can happen in three years. And it could be fun. Great theater: crewcut Digger missionaries going home to Duluth to subvert the Explorer Scouts and turn-on the girl next door and dig themselves.

Tim Leary's not worried. "Those kids will never fit back into the machine," he said recently, "because they have been bent."

TRANSCENDING THE GENERATION GAP

If Allen Ginsberg can get along with his father, there's no excuse for a generation gap. That might have been the hypothesis for a remarkable family meeting on the stage of the Brooklyn Academy of Music.

It was no more than a hypothesis as the poetry reading began. Even after years of rapport, Louis and Allen Ginsberg seem to relish the prospect of a confrontation before an audience. Candor and temper are family traits, and ideologically the gap between the two poets is a gulf.

They are so dissimilar in so many ways, yet they are very much alike. An hour into the reading, it became obvious that the dilemma was solved. The Ginsbergs don't try to bridge any generation gap. They transcend it.

The man who introduced the poets set the tone of the evening when he announced that Louis Ginsberg would read first because he came first. Mr. Ginsberg, who had taught English at Patterson Central High School for the past thirty-eight years, has published two volumes of poetry, and has contributed his work to more than ninety anthologies and magazines. He is a traditionalist, almost Victorian in his care, and is widely recognized as a master of the pun.

He began with a story about some poets who went to the country to try to turn a farmer on to the pleasures of their poems. The farmer would have none of it, Ginsberg said. "What can these city fellows tell us about the pleasures of poultry?" As the audience laughed and groaned, the poet added, "I thought that was a fowl remark."

Like a vaudeville veteran leading up to his thing, Mr. Ginsberg went on to muse about the state of the union (which Lyndon Johnson was simultaneously considering on network television). "You know," he began, "America used to be a melting pot. Now it's a pressure cooker." He talked about finding "a calculated Rusk" in his newspaper at breakfast. "Madison Avenue wants us to buy things we don't want," he lamented, "with money we don't have, to impress people we don't like." And still more puns: "When things pile up but don't add up, I take milk of amnesia." "If we don't watch out, we may all have the right to be cremated equal." There was laughter and applause and Mr. Ginsberg went on to read his poetry.

Louis Ginsberg is a gentle observer. He is a celebrant of the quiet times in life. The purpose he defined is a modest one: "to preserve some fleeting joys and make them permanent." His poetry reflects his eye, and his eye falls upon the odd turns of a simple existence that gracefully spans decades. Mr. Ginsberg notices the little man. "He appeared in the telephone book but not in *Who's Who*," he read from "Epitaph for Mr. Anonymous." "He dropped out of high school because the teachers were interfering with his education." He read a poem about adolescent romance in his English class, and told a story about how he was challenged by a surgeon to describe an operation in verse. Mr. Ginsberg did, and read the result.

His last poem was about a tree and its roots. "It seems that sometimes a poem knows its business better than the poet," Mr. Ginsberg said. "And then it's like the poet feels some force moving his pen. It doesn't happen often, but it happened with this poem."

The poem begins with the poet musing on the roots of a huge tree. As his son might meditate on the sound of a mantra, surrendering to explore the inner space of the sound and its source, so did Louis Ginsberg muse on the tree's great roots, four decades ago, before his son Allen was born, likewise surrendering to search for the source. And then Mr. Ginsberg had visions and the roots came out the other side and curled out into the universe. The poem was a trip. Another level of deep rapport between father and son became obvious.

Allen began his turn with a few minutes of "Hare Krishna" mantra, accompanying himself on a harmonium, and then spoke of his father. "This common consciousness between me and my father puzzles me," he said. "It probably puzzles you. The ground of consciousness is the same ground." And Allen began to read "a parallel poem through the same ground of consciousness" which he wrote last July in Wales while he was on LSD. He was in his father's footsteps.

The younger Ginsberg read poems that he wrote during his travels around the world in 1960, and finished with a "Pentagon Exorcism Mantra" dating from the Pentagon ceremonies of October 21, 1967. Then he talked about the state of the union.

"I'm getting scared because of police state purposes in this country," he said. "A lot of things I imagined in 'Howl' are unfortunately coming through: Moloch hydrogen cloud."

Allen went on to recall LeRoi Jones's case, as evidence of his fears, repeating his belief that Jones was framed. Ginsberg has been working on uniting poets in support of Jones, and plans to take the issue of his trial before the anticensorship committee of PEN, the international literary society, of which he is a member. "LeRoi didn't have any pistols," Ginsberg insisted. "I talked to his father and his wife and they both told me that LeRoi had told them in private that he didn't have any guns. I called California the other day to get people to sign the petition and found that Ferlinghetti and Baez were in jail. And now Spock. Everything has gotten serious in a very weird way. Something serious is going on that we're not psychically ready to recognize."

Louis Ginsberg strolled up to the microphone. "It could be I agree with Allen," he said, "but on LeRoi Jones I want to suspend judgment. He hates the white man. Someone asked him about the three civil rights workers who were killed in the South, and he said, 'Oh, those are artifacts.' Now I can't accept that. The poem in *Evergreen*, telling people to steal and to loot. Those are the cries of a madman.

"I'm going to suspend judgment about his being framed," Mr. Ginsberg said again. "Allen is investigating it.

"One thing I want to say," he continued. "Allen goes to extremes. We are a democracy. We allow people to say, 'LBJ, how many have you killed today?' We have inner resources. These things will level off.

"Guevara, for instance. Without taking sides. Guevara is killed. To Allen, the sky is falling in. Like Ducky-Wucky, Goosey-Loose."

Allen interrupted to offer some substance to the bitterness of LeRoi Jones. "LeRoi's grandfather was in Republican politics in Newark," Ginsberg said. "Once he tried to move the Negro vote over to a reform candidate, and he was killed.

"Jones has broken the mold of consciousness and is working on things around him. I argue with him but we have common ground. It's the legality that's in question. His poems are irrelevant to the determination of fact. But in Russia they don't find poems irrelevant. Jones's trial and the trials of the Soviet writers are precise parallels. I'm worried about the inability of America to recognize the erosion of the legal structure. To take the testimony of the Newark police over LeRoi Jones—who is one of our greatest visionary poets—is shocking."

"What is visionary?" the elder Ginsberg retorted. "To exhort people to steal, to kill? That's not visionary, it's destructive. If LeRoi Jones is to hold all the whites guilty, then we'll have to hold all the Germans guilty. What's past is past. Nothing is done by invoking anarchy, by increasing hatred."

"We need some attempt to communicate information to elders," the younger poet observed to the audience, "to tell them that business as usual no longer serves. The business of America is business! The medium is the message! The Defense Department is the largest business, and the feedback is something incredible. How do we get out of this psychotic state?"

"As long as the generation gap has been brought up," Louis Ginsberg interjected, "I'd like to make an attempt to bridge it." He went on to express reservations about the use of psychedelic drugs, and said that they lead to inactivity.

"All the people at the Pentagon!" Allen yelled. "They were all heads! They weren't inactive!"

"Those who take LSD get blinded," his father replied, speaking metaphorically, I think. "The point is that drugs are a crutch and I say we should use the imagination and fantasy rather than using drugs and blinding ourselves."

It looked like a stalemate. Time for a pun. "They want pot in every chicken," Louis Ginsberg declared, and the audience cheered.

There was a pause, and a nervous kid who looked as though he were in college stood up in the audience. "Allen, Allen," he read from a sheet of paper. "Welcome to Brooklyn!" He and his friends were trying to start a newspaper. "Can you help us?" he asked. "Can you bless us? Oh Krishna!"

"Why not," Ginsberg replied. "Anyone can bless."

So the questions began: "Why are you both poets?"

"Why does fire burn?" the elder Ginsberg asked back. "There's something in our genetic makeup that makes us unburden ourselves in poetry."

"If Jones wasn't carrying guns, why not?" a voice demanded.

Allen went back into the details of the case, and said again that Jones's wife and father assured him that there were no guns.

"Would you expect his wife to say anything against him?" Louis Ginsberg retorted.

Allen mentioned several New York newspaper reporters who, he said, believed Jones's story.

"Why didn't all the reporters say that?" his father asked. "Are they liars?"

"Yes!" roared the audience.

"They'd get fired!" Allen yelled.

A lady stood up. "What was that you were singing at the beginning?" she asked Allen.

Ginsberg said that he was singing a mantra, or a magic verbal formula, and said it was the "Hare Krishna" mantra, or the Maha Mantra—Great Mantra—for this age, and that it was supposed to be able to change the universe, and that the Beatles were digging it.

"Does that explain it?" he asked the lady.

"No," she said. "It sounds like an affectation."

"Further reasons," Ginsberg continued. "It's an exercise in breathing, a form of yoga I do practice, and public chanting is especially recommended."

"What do you mean, magical chant?" she persisted.

Allen Ginsberg moved back to the podium where his harmonium sat, and he began to pump it, and it began to drone, and, as his father sat back in a chair to rest, the bearded bard breathed deeply and began to sing. "Hare Om Namos Shivaye," he sang. "Hare Om Namos Shivaye."

LEATHER IS IN, LOVE; FLOWERS ARE OUT

A LONG WAY FROM MAY TO DECEMBER

The hippies are dead and the Diggers may be dying. A year ago, neither word had yet appeared in the pages of *The New York Times*. In twelve months the Lower East Side went through changes unprecedented in its constantly changing history. Many will be hard to forget: the Be-Ins, the Sweep-In, the Smoke-Ins, the free music, the free dope, the Free Store; the Diggers, the dealers, the deaths. Others are already forgotten. Chief among the forgotten changes are the valiant attempts at community organization, some of which lasted a week, none of which survive today. In the first fresh days of a new year, it seems somehow appropriate to recall some of these attempts. Some may be meat for resolutions.

The Jade Companions of the Flower Dance, the first evidence of cohesion in the hippie community, was incorporated after a series of community meetings to administer a bail fund and maintain an emergency telephone. Several thousand membership cards with a Mayan motif were printed to be sold at $5.00 apiece. Several were sold. The Jade Companions opened its headquarters at Ed Sanders' Peace Eye Bookstore in the spring and, Captain Fink being in the early stages of his enlightenment, closed several weeks later in a blitz of police harassment. The bail fund functioned for only a short time, but its legend lingered on, and flower children collected small change in the streets throughout the summer, incanting its name. As the legend itself grew stale, they turned to panhandling.

The East Village Showcase was established in the spring with the aid of the Department of Parks to encourage the use of Tompkins Square Park by presenting entertainment in the bandshell. In the aftermath of the Memorial Day clash, where seventy riot-trained TPF cops broke up a hippie picnic with nightsticks, the Showcase continued its presentations undaunted, attracting great numbers to the tense area. In the middle of a set by a folk-rock group, a group of Puerto Ricans came to the bandshell and demanded Latin music. Rejected by the master of ceremonies, they started swinging. The music stopped. An iron curtain rattled down to close the stage. In minutes, an angry mob had formed and the helmeted TPF returned to the scene, clearing the park and sealing it off for the night. The next day, the Showcase got the shaft from the Parks Department, and the park listened to Latin music all day, thanks to a phonograph hooked up to the PA system.

The East Village Defense Committee was established in the middle of the Tompkins Square maelstrom, envisioned as an "umbrella" organization to oversee and coordinate the various projects in the hippie community which were then stumbling under way. During the committee's second meeting, while the defenders debated who would man an emergency temporary telephone, the TPF returned to Tompkins Square Park to squelch the mob of Puerto Ricans who had squelched the East Village Showcase. By the time the emergency telephone dilemma was resolved, it was all over. The defenders learned this the next morning, and the East Village Defense Committee faded away.

The East Village Ad Hoc Committee for Community Action was introduced by a press release a few weeks later. The paper explained that the committee "has been formed in order to serve as a functional apparatus for communication and responsible response to the community's needs during the summer. The need for such a committee has been obvious. There has been no cohesive program of action. Rather there has developed a myriad of splintered reactions by organizations and leaders with overlapping aims. . . . Perhaps the Lower East Side is presently involved in the 'quiet riot' in history but we refuse to allow the first blood to be innocent blood due to a 'power vacuum' with the blind leading the blind." The press release was the last I heard from them.

The True Light Beavers, a small band of intergalactic nomads who built shrines of garbage and wore True Light Beaver tee-shirts, issued one handbill declaring "There are no problems, there are only things to be done," and immediately disbanded.

Love to the True Light Beavers.

EXIT DIGGERS

It seemed to be another of a series of lurid torture cases which caused a mild ripple of shock across a numb public consciousness. Here was the *Daily News* account:

On Tuesday afternoon, [Kenneth] Goss went to a sort of communal pad at 723 East 6th Street to visit a friend he called Roland. . . . The flat Goss visited used to be a hippie hangout. Roland wasn't in. Goss said he got into a fight with another youth whom he knew only as "Gypsy" or "Hillbilly." He kicked a knife out of the youth's hand, he said. The two decided to stop fighting and shake hands.

Goss went back to the flat at 9 p.m. The gang assault then started, he said. After he was punched and kicked for about two hours, he was taken to a building on East 10th Street—he didn't remember the address—which had formerly been operated by the Diggers, a hippie charity group. He said he was tortured and beaten because gang rules decree if you fight one member you fight them all.

He was held there until 6 a.m. Wednesday, suffering kicks and blows and other abuses. He was taken to the Avenue B flat (where the eight persons were subsequently arrested) where he was burned with cigarettes and doused with a roach killing liquid. He was beaten and bound. On Thursday, when he was finally left alone, he picked up a knife which may have been purposely dropped at his side by a girl, and cut himself loose, and escaped.

He went to the East 5th Street police station and told his story.

Goss told the *News* that "when he first reported his experience to the police, they laughed at him." One of the arresting officers told the *News*, "At first we were skeptical, but the kid holds to his story and we're sure it's true."

Perhaps there is a case for trusting a cop's instincts. A week later, as the story was resolved in unparalleled irony, all charges were dismissed against the eight persons after, the *Post* reported on page 17, "The grand jury heard the medical background of the accuser, Kenneth Goss, 20, described by officials at Central Islip State Hospital on Long Island as a pathological liar known to inflict burns on himself." Goss was placed in the Bellevue psychiatric ward, in which he had been first confined in 1957.

It had been rough enough on the eight persons who were arrested. It is true that they are bikers. They are members of a shadowy subculture where privacy is preservation, where publicity is disaster. The investigation during the week when they were imprisoned revealed that one of the eight had a warrant out for his arrest. He remains in jail today. Their cover was blown; their identities titillated the masses. Victims of an unspeakable fraud, they spent a week in the Tombs and then were released, without compensation, or, one assumes, apology.

But they were not the only victims. The Digger Free Store, which still occupied a storefront at 264 East 10th Street, was implicated in the original *News* article. It was, to say the least, the worst kind of publicity.

I went to the Digger Free Store three days after the bikers were released. The apartment upstairs, which, when I had visited it two weeks before, seemed to be a thriving operation with forty kids waiting for a dinner which was steaming on the stoves, was now vacant.

Downstairs in the store I found the several people who had managed the Digger operation after Ritchie split sitting dejected on old piles of clothing and mattresses. Their landlord had just given them the final eviction notice, which was to be effective at midnight.

The Diggers, who have asked me not to use their names, began a story that would last for four hours.

The story begins with the exit of Ritchie and Suzi and Clyde who, backed by $1,000.00 from the Community Breast, a nonprofit corporation set up after a successful benefit in the summer to channel funds for community development on the East Side, brought the Free Store to life on September 21. Ritchie set the tone for the store. He was a veteran biker from San Francisco, a rip-snorting, gasoline-alley Digger, whose greatest moment was when he was invited to join the Hell's Angels. (Recent rumors report that Ritchie is back on the Coast and flying Angel colors, apparently having accepted the invitation.) Suzi was Ritchie's old lady, who came from Detroit to San Francisco, where she made the scene in Haight-Ashbury and met Ritchie, and then came with Ritchie from San Francisco to New York, in flight from a collection of traffic tickets that threatened Ritchie with prison. And Clyde was a tough, young punk from New Orleans, who first met Ritchie in San Francisco and joined him in New York, where he was partially tamed by fame and an angel from the Group Image.

Ritchie had reportedly managed the Digger Free Store in Haight-Ashbury and, because of his rare experience, he was welcomed on the East Side as someone who might get the floundering notion of a Free Store off the ground. Ritchie had a great Digger routine, flavored with ominous aggression, and in a blitz of squandering funds and compulsive work, he and Suzi and Clyde got the Free Store to function. When the original money from the Community Breast, spent on lumber, rent, fixtures, and Ritchie's motorcycle, ran out, various individual donors and a series of benefits at Steve Paul's Scene kept the Free Store running until Ritchie split on November 16.

The motorcycle aura of violence which characterized the Free Store during Ritchie's two-month reign seemed to antagonize and intimidate not only his backers but much of the surrounding neighborhood. "Violence was the whole theme," a Provo recalled. "Violence was the whole pattern of the Free Store. They were hung on violence. When people came in and bugged Ritchie, he responded by trying to kill them."

The last time that I saw Ritchie in the Free Store was a few days before I left for the West Coast in early October. At that time—two weeks after the store had opened—the Free Store was thriving. It seemed that the Diggers had established a good relationship with the residents on the block. Puerto Rican street leaders were working in the store.

But, shortly thereafter, the store's relationship with the street deteriorated, finally to the point where the store was under siege with barrages of bricks coming through the windows, which the Diggers allegedly countered with posting riflemen on the roof.

There wasn't much left of the Free Store at that point. Begun as a service, it had come to be hated by its neighbors. It was a thorn in the side of a ghetto. The windows were broken, the stock was depleted, and its backers had decided that it should be closed. But the remaining Diggers, who were Ritchie's successors in spirit and fact, wanted to keep the store open. "We figured, why leave the store," they said. "Let's rebuild it."

It was at this point when several people now affiliated with ESSO, the East Side Service Organization, became involved in the Free Store. ESSO was still on the drawing board at the time—it has recently been incorporated—and was envisioned by neighborhood activists such as Abbie Hoffman as a multifaceted service organization involved with fund-raising, communication, and a general fusion of energy and matter. Hoffman had been involved with the planning and packing of the Free Store from the start, and it now seemed that the Free Store would be an appropriate project for ESSO to undertake.

"ESSO came in," the Diggers recalled. "They said, we'll supply the funds. They wanted the front room of the apartment as an office. They explained a bunch of good things for us. We were short of money and we fell for it. All we ever saw was $100.00 for wood."

At this time, the store was closed and the Diggers were living and working in an apartment on the first floor of the same building. The Diggers were primarily concerned about the functioning of the apartment, which served as an emergency crash pad and a free kitchen for kids from the street. ESSO, on the other hand, was concerned about redesigning and reopening the store and, most especially, finding a base on which to get the rest of their envisioned project under way. Their conceptions conflicted. While the Diggers sought to raise money for free food, ESSO began to rebuild the store. Neither was concerned about the other's project, and each later accused the other of lack of effort.

The Diggers said that they put up their personal money

to keep the store and apartment going, but that they finally had reached a dead end. "It got to the point where ESSO had to come through," they said.

The Diggers said that people from ESSO had agreed to sign a new lease on the store on Monday, December 11, the day the *Daily News* story on the Goss case broke. When they came to the store, the Diggers recalled, they were concerned about the article. "They said that we needed some good publicity," the Diggers recalled. "They said that we would have a meeting at the store Tuesday morning."

On local television Monday night, a shot of the Digger Free Store appeared in connection with a report on the Goss case.

"On Tuesday, ESSO pulled out," the Diggers said. "They said, 'Sorry, the store's closed.' They said that we were a bad risk. They said, 'You've always had a bad name.' Three hours later the landlord came down and said that we had to be out by midnight. They had canceled the lease without even telling us. He said that he would lock the store and the apartment by midnight." The Diggers persuaded the landlord to give them a few days in which to try to raise the bread for the rent.

"One day after the *Daily News* story broke, we got the royal screw from ESSO," the Diggers said, "from people whom we have always thought above intimidation by the *News*. It just puts eight people who have been working their asses off into the street."

It appears that some people affiliated with ESSO believed the *Daily News* report that the Diggers and the Free Store were involved in the Goss case. If they did, they were right. That is to say that the Diggers were deeply involved in the incident, a false version of which appeared in the *News*. If ESSO had been primarily concerned about the detrimental publicity surrounding the incident, they had good reason to be. The sensational accounts of the Goss case had reached such nightmarish proportions that it seemed that no amount of "setting the record straight" could ever correct the original impression. Here is the story which the Diggers told me, and which they said that they had told to ESSO before the organization pulled out of the store:

The Diggers said that around noon on Tuesday, November 30, Kenneth Goss went to the apartment on the sixth floor of a tenement at 723 East 6th Street, which had formerly been operated by the Diggers as a crash pad. Goss found a fifteen-year-old boy, known only as "Gunner," in the apartment. "Kenny thought he might be an informer," the Diggers said, "and he felt free to indispose him." A fight ensued, the Diggers said, and "Gunner" sustained four rib fractures, probably permanent kidney damage, multiple head injuries, and possible brain damage. The Diggers said that "Gunner" was taken to Bellevue Hospital that afternoon. They said that he was a runaway and has since been sent home to his parents.

At midnight, the Diggers went to the apartment on East 6th Street and brought Goss back to the Free Store. "We were planning on taking him to the police station," the Diggers said, "but we decided not to because it wasn't right to turn anybody in." Goss remained at the store until 4 a.m. Friday morning. "Nothing happened to Goss at the store or the crash pad," the Diggers said. "At that point there were twenty people crashing here. There was no room to maim him."

Friday morning, the Diggers sent Goss to the apartment on Avenue B which the police would visit nine days later. "A friend needed somebody to clean up the apartment and wash the dishes in exchange for a place to crash," the Diggers said, "so we sent him over there." Goss stayed at the apartment for five days, leaving the following Tuesday. The Diggers conceded that Goss might have been harassed at the apartment on Avenue B, "but nothing you could call torture," and they stressed that he stayed there of his own free will. One of the Diggers saw Goss three days later and told him to get out of town.

At 1 p.m. on Saturday, December 9, the Diggers said, "a spade cat named Mr. White came to the Free Store with Goss and another guy in a 1967 yellow Chevrolet. Mr. White hit a guy and a chick on the sidewalk in front of the Free Store. He said that the store was an evil influence in the black community. He said that he'd get the Diggers. He promised that there would never be another Free Store."

Saturday night Goss and two members of the Ninth Precinct's "hippie squad" came to a party at the apartment on Avenue B. Goss pointed out the eight people who were arrested. The police claimed to have seized a cache of amphetamine and LSD in the apartment, as well as an arsenal which included 265 rounds of ammunition, three rifles, a sawed-off shotgun, a bayonet, a machete, a butcher knife, and handcuffs. A photograph in the *Daily News* showed a detective fondling the butcher knife.

(*The New York Times* reported on December 16 "that charges of possession of narcotics lodged against the eight persons released yesterday had been dropped when laboratory tests proved that the substances seized . . . were not narcotics. Authorities also decided that a so-called arsenal of weapons found at the site were not linked to the defendants.")

On Monday, December 11, the story of the arrests broke in the local press. On Tuesday, the Diggers faced eviction.

The Diggers were plagued all week with a series of obscene phone calls. On Tuesday, one of the Diggers received the following unsigned letter:

> You know me very well but I can't tell you who I am because of what I am going to tell you. But you are in great danger. I was told that some guys are getting paid to kill you. So if I were you I'd get out of here as fast as you can. Also told that [name deleted] and the Diggers aren't going to be very long. And if I told you's what they said that they are going to get me too for telling you. I don't want to see this happen. So Be Ware of this. I love you all.

On Saturday, December 16, the Free Store died. The landlord kicked the remaining Diggers out into the street, and he said that he was calling the Salvation Army to pick up the remaining Free Stock. One of the Diggers destroyed what was left of the store with chains. I doubt if napalm could have done a more thorough job. They tore down the "LOVE" sign over the door, replaced it with "HATE" and split.

The group of Diggers remains intact, at least to the extent of occasional meetings and hopes for a commune. They want to quietly work to build a base of operations which they hope will begin to function in the spring. Right now they only want to fade out.

The Diggers still harbor some bitterness toward ESSO. "They call themselves Diggers," one said. "Where were they when the crash pad on 6th Street was busted and forty-seven people moved into the store? Where were they when we needed food? Where were they when the bricks started coming through the windows?"

The answer is that they were not there because they had no reason to become concerned and involved.

The obvious heroes of the Diggers are the bikers, who have recently come en masse to the East Side. "The bikers helped us when no one else would," the Diggers said.

"These were the guys when the bricks were coming through the windows—these were the guys who were out there catching them. They caught them in their teeth.

"We're not talking about the sidewalk commandos. They've got no class. They're not righteous. A biker is a guy who doesn't bullshit, who knows what's going on."

I spoke with a member of the ESSO board who explained to me his conception of the history of the Free Store. ESSO's position on various issues is the sum of the positions of its individual members. The organization has by definition no leaders and no spokesmen.

"We went through a period of paranoia this fall," he said. "The murders were the symbol of it. Ritchie and Galahad were two victims of that paranoia.

"Ritchie's conception was that the Puerto Rican wants your old lady and either you're going to give them your old lady or you're going to hit them with a chain. Ritchie was on a San Francisco Hell's Angel trip in New York. That trip isn't accepted here. If you stay in New York, you confront the impossibilities, but not the tire chains.

"Our involvement in the Free Store was a mistake from the beginning. We put ourselves in the position of money giver and helping them with plans. It couldn't work. We had three or four meetings on the store. Some of our artists were involved in the planning of the store. We were going to have an office upstairs with a phone. This was mad. ESSO is ESSO. It's not a Free Store.

"We made a mistake. It was an old-form action we did. We were looking in the rear-view mirror. How do you remedy a mistake? You remedy a mistake by pulling out. That's all right. We won't do that anymore.

"Our goal is to change and affect the environment. Our goal is to get energy together with matter. Things we should do down here are like getting one hundred people down to the Ninth Precinct to turn themselves in as runaways when a crash pad is busted. Or like having a big street festival at the end of January. It will have street theater and destruction artists, and flatbed trucks going around all the blocks, and processions, and a huge bonfire in Tompkins Square Park. It will have rock bands and Puerto Rican bands. It will be a gigantic celebration that will involve all the blocks. It will be a gigantic celebration of the wintertime.

"It's theater and it's revolution. The revolution is freedom. If we want to be joyful at the end of the revolution, then we have to be joyful in the middle of the revolution —keeping in mind the impossibility.

"This trip has no leaders, no spokesmen, because it's revolutionary. I'm not saying that planning doesn't go on, but the planning is just to ignite. After it's ignited, it sustains itself. What we're out of is ideology now, because ideology is an ego trip.

"The cops have gotta be confronted. Fink is the ambassador of the Establishment on the Lower East Side, and we've gotta stone that embassy. There are all sorts of ways of throwing stones, one of which is really throwing stones.

"Then there's the Psychedelic Mafia, part of ESSO that's involved with beautiful paintings and exorcisms, like The War Is Over thing. The painting involves more than paint. The painting was fused with people going up Fifth Avenue chanting "The war is over." The painting has got to be fused with the confrontation of the impossibility. One of the things that ESSO is, is that fusion. It's an incorporated myth. It's the fusion that means revolution, New York style.

"It does not involve being somebody's boss. The octopus is an old-form organism. Even if it momentarily hurts a few kids' feelings, the legs of the octopus have to be cut off. We didn't run at the smell of motorcycles. The kids set up the paranoia that we were out to run the store."

The ESSO member recalled a meeting held at the Welfare Building on Avenue B around the end of November. The meeting, attended by Puerto Rican gang leaders, the Free Store Diggers, members of the ESSO board, and members of various community projects, resulted in a "peace treaty" among the Puerto Rican gangs and between the gangs and other elements of the community. It was considered a milestone in the evolution of the East Side.

A few weeks after the meeting, the ESSO member recalled an incident at the Diggers' crash pad on East 6th Street. Someone threw a beer can out of the sixth floor window, which narrowly missed some Puerto Ricans in the street. The Puerto Ricans went up to inquire about the can, and the Diggers responded by swinging chains. The key gang leader who negotiated the peace treaty was in jail, and the East Side almost blew up over the incident.

"If anybody was freaked by anything," he said, "it wasn't the newspaper accounts of the Goss case. It was that. You don't take a chain up somebody's head because you threw a beer can out a window.

"That doesn't give you any freedom. You put yourself in slavery to paranoia. You put yourself in slavery to dissension inside the community. That's why Fink and the ambassadors won. That's why the embassy won.

"There were two main problems with the Free Store," he said. "ESSO and the Free Store were two seeds that germinated at the same time. The plants got their vines crossed. The problem was whether or not to lose the life force. It wasn't giving money but losing sap.

"Here were people who grew from the street. They had to realize that not only did they have to do the Free Store for the street, but they had to live with the street. If ESSO and the Free Store were joined, they would keep fighting with the street, and that would screw us up.

"That's the first problem, the minor problem.

"The other problem is that ESSO would be killed if it were involved in the running of anything. That is an old form. ESSO is a new form.

"It was a decision that had to be made immediately. The decision was made in too severe a way. Very bad consequences came of it. We would have had to make a very subtle decision, and it's hard for subtlety to come out of that drastic a situation."

It was as if there were two Free Stores in the same space, and when the one with the money decided to close, the other was left hanging. It is clear that the partnership was a mistake from the beginning. ESSO had no alternative but to end it.

The tragedy, of course, is the wasted energy. The kids had a surplus of energy. It might have been directed; as it was, it was allowed to spin off, a process which came to be destructive. In retrospect, we can all see what should have been done. The Free Store should have been, and it could have been, independent. Funds were always available from other sources.

Without direction, the Free Store evolved into a bummer. As a last resort, ESSO brought it down. Shortly before the Goss incident, the apartment above the Free Store seemed to be finally functioning. Was it evolving out of the bummer? No one will know.

Each side indicts the other. ESSO's action is clear, but is there redemption for the Diggers? They are painted as a clique of motorcycle hoods. They were clearly fallible. They were considered exploiters.

I have wondered why, if the kids were such exploiters, they ever bothered with the complexities of a free store. Were they in the store frankly as exploiters, taking advantage of a free place to crash and the cream of the stock? I spoke with them at length, and I don't believe they were.

Was it instead an ego game? The Diggers were the heroes of the bike-oriented street kids. Was their commitment only a scene, based on a shallow philosophy which could be implemented or discarded at will? Or was there something more?

The Diggers in the Free Store impressed me as kids who had evolved into social action from the street. With the possible exception of the Provos, this has never happened before in the new community on the East Side. I saw in them for the first time a possibility of bridging the critical gap between the leadership and the street on the East Side. Unfortunately, the gap is still with us.

The gap must be bridged. The action has only been postponed. We will face it again and then, like the Free Store, it will be a revolutionary, evolutionary experiment, which is bound to be turbulent. There is too much energy around to enjoy passive change.

THE POLITICS OF GARBAGE

The lights were set up in the small tenement commune last Tuesday and the cameras were ready. The film crew was set to shoot and there was a knock at the door.

A cameraman opened the door. Three men walked into the kitchen. "They didn't look like cops," Peter Gessner, who was directing the documentary, recalled. "They were tough, young guys in sportclothes. They had little beards. I thought one might be the super."

Gessner started the cameras and turned on his tape recorder as the men went to the two youngest kids in the room and asked them to step outside into the hall. "They didn't show any badges," Gessner said. "They didn't have a search warrant. It had the aura of a shakedown."

In the hall the detectives identified themselves and told the two kids—whom they judged to be runaways—that they would be taken to the Ninth Precinct station. The ten people remaining in the apartment prepared to come along.

"We're going down to the precinct," the cop said into the tape recorder. "Don't do anything to cause problems."

Ignoring the warning, the kids called the PTA—a new

neighborhood group of Protestors, Terrorists, and Anarch-
ists—and followed the cops and their friends to the station.

The kids were waiting in front of the desk at the Ninth
Precinct at 10:15 p.m. when the PTA arrived. The PTA
and the kids went outside to regroup. The problem, they
reasoned, was one of definition. After all, they were all
runaways, from something. The cops were just discrimi-
nating against runaways under eighteen.

Now thirty-five strong, they returned to the station and
turned themselves in as guilty runaways. Rejected, they
sat on the floor. Deputy Inspector Joseph Fink arrived.
An argument ensued. There was no obvious leader, so
police arrested one kid for playing a guitar and another
kid for dancing in the shadow of the desk sergeant's desk.
Both were charged with disorderly conduct. The PTA
and the remaining kids went outside to regroup again.

It was a genuine confrontation, genuine enough to call
Fink back to the station on a Tuesday night, genuine
enough to move the aroused demonstrators to the sidewalk across the street from the station. There was one
sign: "JUSTICE IS DENIED UNTIL YOU'RE 18 AND THEN IT'S
DEAD." There was an apparent backlash as a volley of
eggs hurled from a window overhead exploded around
the kids in the street. The station was shielded from the
demonstrators by a line of mysterious paddy-wagons. One
kid attacked the barricade with a spray can of white
paint. He was arrested for criminal mischief after he
painted "COPS SUCK" on the second paddy-wagon.

By now the PTA had arrived in modest force, and it was
time to stimulate the deaf ears of the opposition. Suddenly a shout: "Let's block off Second Avenue!"

Now for a little action. The crowd rushed to Second

Avenue, half a block away, and suddenly garbage cans were crashing across cobblestones, trash flying in headlight beams, cans and lids and rotten vegetables bounding over hoods and into car doors. Cabs swerved and kids cheered. Stacks of garbage, two-day piles, everything, everything, into the street. They scored twenty-five cans in twice as many seconds and then built a makeshift barricade across St. Mark's Place, halting the astounded traffic. It was a spree. The PTA was ecstatic.

They circled back down Second Avenue. Motorists on St. Mark's Place left their cars to move the cans. Second Avenue was full of garbage and not a sign of cops.

Suddenly they noticed a tall, blond kid out in the middle of the street, dodging cars and dumping strewn garbage back into the cans. The PTA was horrified. The kid dragged a can back to the sidewalk. The PTA approached him.

"What are you doing?" the PTA protested. "You can't do that."

"If you want to go stone the police station," the kid replied, "go do it. Don't take it out on these people."

"It's a political act," the PTA persisted. "The whole society is the enemy. Not just the police."

"I don't see how you're going to end repression by being repressive," the kid said, and he started scraping up the trash with a garbage can lid. A police car moved up slowly.

"Don't go out there," the PTA warned. "They're going to hurt you." The kid kept scraping up the garbage and the police moved on.

The kids picked up some of the refilled cans and a few they missed on the first round and hurled them back into the street. Three patrolmen rounded the corner of St.

Mark's Place and looked on aghast as the cans flew into the street. They raised their nightsticks and went hurtling toward the kids. The kids saw them coming and took off. The lead cop lunged at the last kid with his stick, hitting him in the ass. And the kids disappeared.

Two young Puerto Ricans stood on the curb and wondered at the strewn garbage. "Look at this, man," one said. "It looks like a gang war."

"Crazy hippies," the other sighed.

The kids and the PTA regrouped in front of the precinct station. The media had arrived. "Hey, that's ABC!" a kid shouted as a network news car pulled up. Soon the lights were on again and the documentary resumed. The first thing the network cameras shot was the aforementioned graffiti on the second paddy-wagon. And then the paddy-wagons were driven off.

The crowd was involved in another strategy session. "Listen," a kid said, "with all the media here, why don't we all get arrested. You know, walk in single file."

"We already tried that," another said.

The cameramen began to shoot the strategy session and a forest of erect middle fingers arose. The media were foiled.

The crowd then went to the door of the station, now guarded by seven cops, and asked to hold a meeting which they said Fink had agreed to earlier. One cop said that Fink had gone home. The kids persisted, and the cop agreed to let one kid enter. The others insisted on sending two representatives. The meeting was stalemated.

Fink came out. "What meeting?" he asked. "I never agreed to a mass meeting. I agreed to meet with representatives."

"We have no representatives," said a voice from the crowd. Fink shrugged.

"We say, look, let the kids out and we'll talk,' said another voice. Fink smiled.

"If they arrest the runaways and break down our doors," another voice threatened, "we'll fuck up the street, that's all." Fink said that the runaways weren't under arrest, they were only being detained, and he said that the detectives had been invited into the apartment. "They're not in jail," he said. "The brother of one is coming to take him home."

"He'll be back next week," someone shouted. Fink shrugged.

"They've busted six pads this week and it's gotta stop," another voice said. "Every time they bust another pad it gets worse."

"Take it to the Civilian Review Board," said Deputy Inspector Fink.

"Captain Fink," Abbie Hoffman pleaded, "you're doing a bad thing. If you close the communes, you'll have kids running loose in the street with no place to sleep."

"They can sleep here," Fink smiled.

"Is that an invitation for kids to sleep in jail?" Abbie asked, astounded.

"Yes," Fink said. The crowd cheered, but they didn't believe it. "You can sleep at Abbie's house," Fink added, as an afterthought. The kids grumbled, but Fink was paternal.

"You're making a lot of noise," he said. "You had better go home while you're ahead."

The press packed their cameras and the kids wandered off, complaining loudly, and the PTA mused enchanted at what they hoped was a catalyst. It was past midnight, and soon they would sleep, perchance to dream of flying garbage cans.

PICKETS PROTEST PROFITS

"Hey, lady. You going to the Diamond Ball?"

"Lookit the fancy lady going to the Diamond Ball!"

Jeers and whistles. The elderly woman, dressed in an ancient red velvet coat that fell almost to her ankles, glanced, frightened, at her hecklers and hurried past Bergdorf-Goodman to cross Fifth Avenue. She obviously wasn't going to the Diamond Ball, an annual charity dance of the highest calibre held last Wednesday night at the Plaza Hotel, but her faded grandeur was enough to entice a few of the youths who, with decadence on their minds, had come to the Plaza that night to protest what they called the "Festival of the Vultures."

The "vultures" included Vice-President and Mrs. Hubert Humphrey, Governor and Mrs. Nelson Rockefeller, Mr. and Mrs. Charles W. Englehard (whose holdings include South African diamond mines, Newark slums, and a close association with President Johnson), Mr. and Mrs. Jack Valenti, Senator Mike Mansfield, Roger Lewis (president of General Dynamics), Marietta Tree, George D. Woods (recently replaced by Robert McNamara as President of the World Bank), Senator and Mrs. John Sherman Cooper, Mr. and Mrs. Paul Newman, and the Baroness Jacqueline de Guinzberg.

Their would-be tormentors, called for convenience the Coalition, represented a militant cluster of antiwar groups which had recently split with the Fifth Avenue Peace Parade Committee in a dispute over tactics. The Coalition includes Youth Against War and Fascism, Veterans and Reservists to End the War in Vietnam, SNCC, U.S. Committee to Aid the NLF, Black Mask, Pageant Players, and six other groups.

Finally there was a contingent of at least five hundred police, called to contain the three hundred demonstrators and ensure that the Diamond Ball would not be rudely disrupted. This they did, by ringing the block around the Plaza with barricades, by inflexibly confronting the demonstrators and denying their right to demonstrate, by seizing every opportunity—a sign or an NLF flag—to provoke or instigate violence, by arresting more than thirty demonstrators on charges ranging from disorderly conduct to resisting arrest, to, in the case of the Pageant Players, masquerading in public, and by striking a running youth on the back of his head with a nightstick, felling him to the pavement with an impressed concussion. The youth, who was not arrested, was taken to Bellevue Hospital, where he was in critical condition.

I stood with a friend on the north side of the Plaza, our backs to the south wall of Central Park, facing the entrance through which the "guests" would pass. Perhaps the only concession to the presence of the demonstrators was the use of the side entrance of the hotel instead of the carriage entrance in front. The Vice-President used this side entrance, an hour after the demonstration had been dispersed.

It was cold that night, and the glittering candles of the Edwardian Room looked warm and inviting. There was a party—perhaps the party—on the second floor, and a gentleman in black tie, a cocktail in his hand, would occasionally stroll to the window and glance down on the barricades, police, and demonstrators in the dark, freezing night.

"The millionaires attending the Diamond Ball," a Coalition handbill read, "are celebrating profits made largely out of the death and destruction of the Vietnam war. They symbolize the imperialist motivation of the war, and many of them are even personally in control of the billionaire corporations that needed war and overseas investment to expand and profit."

A cop walked by whistling "The Caisson Song." The gentleman gazed down from the window. It was too much.

The demonstrators had hoped to exploit the aura of glittering decadence surrounding the festivities at the Plaza. The irony was too inviting; it demanded more than a picket line. The Pageant Players rose to the occasion, and came to the Plaza costumed as the wounded and maimed: men with slings and blood-soaked bandages, hobbling on canes, women as Vietnamese or, alternately, in ragged gowns. They had hoped to confront and disgust the "vultures" at the door, and there was talk of sacks of blood being available to hurl at the socialites, but the police thwarted their plans. The costumed demonstrators were left to roam about the streets, puzzling and entertaining pedestrians.

The police had offered to allow the demonstrators to set

up a line on the sidewalk on the north side of 59th Street facing the Plaza. The leaders of the demonstration rejected the offer because they felt they were defenseless in that position. "There was a wall behind the sidewalk and a fifteen-foot drop into the park," a spokesman for the Coalition explained. "We thought that was the worst area because if the police attacked there was nowhere to move to. We would have been trapped."

So the demonstration was never allowed to form. The police kept the groups of demonstrators apart and in motion. Rumors of containment and mass arrest kept the youths themselves dispersed. If a contingent formed, the police would direct it to another area. If the people were slow to move, the police formed a wall and began to shove. On several occasions, police pushed masses of demonstrators into moving traffic. When demonstrators protested, they were arrested.

The major encounter was early in the evening, when police forced demonstrators northwest across Fifth Avenue to an area above 59th Street. The demonstrators still carried signs and NLF flags. Suddenly a scuffle began in the center of the group and additional police rushed in, swinging nightsticks. The group of demonstrators panicked and ran, chased by police into flanks of more police. Several demonstrators were arrested and, mysteriously, after the encounter no signs or flags were to be seen.

A large contingent decided to circle the block, and walked in a long line along the north side of 59th Street toward Sixth Avenue, were blocked again by police, and formed a picket line, which was dispersed after a few minutes. Another contingent remained three blocks north, along the east side of the Central Park.

The demonstration had been routed. Frustrated, sev-

eral groups of the militants left the area around the Plaza
to work on mobile disruption around midtown, away from
the masses of police. One group went east again to Sixth
Avenue, eventually winding their way down to the re-
cruiting center at Times Square, where they demonstrated until they were again dispersed by the police.
Another group went east on 59th Street, pausing in front
of the Playboy Club to shout "We want peace," to the
intersection at Madison Avenue, where a lone cop was
directing traffic. As others blocked the traffic, a dozen
demonstrators surrounded the cop and began to mimic
his traffic signals. Other demonstrators pulled trash cans
into the intersection to block the cars. The intersection
had been held for several minutes, and traffic backed up
for more than a block, when the demonstrators heard the
roar of a single motorcycle, and jumped aside as the
police cycle hurtled through the crowd. The cars took off,
and the demonstrators ran south to the next intersection,
which they blocked as the light turned. They blocked
each intersection long enough to pull garbage cans into
the street, sometimes dumping their contents. Some demonstrators pounded on the car windows. Others heckled
an occasional black cab driver who tried to pass through
the barricades. On 57th Street, an older man jumped out
of a stalled cab and, as his wife protested, began to swing
at the demonstrators. He was restrained by the traffic
cops.

Then the demonstrators circled back west and continued down Fifth Avenue, halting traffic at each intersection. Now, as they pulled the trash cans into the street,
they set them afire. The obstacles and flames made an
eerie spectacle of Fifth Avenue at night.

There had been no sign of the massive police force

during all the traffic disruptions. Suddenly, between 54th and 55th streets, twenty cops were almost on top of the demonstrators. The youths bolted and ran down Fifth Avenue. The police went after them. On the next block, the lead cop swung at the last kid with his nightstick, hitting him on the back of his head. The youth fell unconscious and bleeding profusely from his mouth.

The police paused to pull the trash cans back to the curb and the demonstrators paused a few blocks down the avenue to continue the disruption. A well-dressed woman stood by the youth who had been felled. "It was horrible," she said. "I saw the whole thing. Who can I complain to? I want to file a complaint."

"Was it a cop?" someone asked.

"Of course it was a cop," she said. "It's horrible. Horrible."

She complained to the police as they returned, but was ignored. The police called an ambulance.

The rest of the demonstrators had abandoned the traffic disruption and now, exhilarated, just ran down the street. They turned into the promenade in Rockefeller Center and ran down toward the skating rink, filled with skaters who, it turned out, were part of a skating party of supporters of Senator Robert Kennedy. On the sidewalk overlooking the rink stood a few people holding signs appealing to Kennedy to declare his candidacy. "BOBBY IN '68" one read. "RFK WILL END THE WAR" read another. The demonstrators waved at the Kennedy people and the Kennedy people waved back. One group of demonstrators remained at the skating rink, where they formed a picket line. Another group ran down 49th Street toward Sixth Avenue.

Few arrests had been made since the demonstrators left

the area around the Plaza. The traffic disruption had been quick and sporadic. With fires burning up Fifth Avenue and traffic in a melée, the police were genuinely provoked. Suddenly a squad car and a paddy wagon rounded the corner of Fifth Avenue and 49th Street. The police pulled up next to the people holding the signs, which faced the rink and could not be read from the street. The police jumped out of the car, roughly seized four of the people, and threw them into the wagon. As the paddy wagon took off, other police tore up the signs, and maintenance men scurried out of the buildings to pick up the remains. The rest of the Kennedy people, apparently oblivious to the incident, continued to skate.

A lone youth stood dazed on the sidewalk as the men picked up the torn signs. "Who are you?" I asked him. "Where are you from?"

"There's been a mistake," he said. "There's been a terrible mistake."

Later that night, the demonstrators who had been arrested were brought into court. They were represented by an attorney from the National Lawyers' Guild. The charges of masquerading which had been placed against five members of the Pageant Players were dismissed. The other twenty-nine demonstrators were charged with disorderly conduct (twenty-six), resisting arrest (four), and a few compounded charges of obstructing vehicular or pedestrian traffic and interfering with an arrest. It seems that the majority of the arrests had been made among the demonstrators who remained to picket at Rockefeller Center. All but the four demonstrators charged with resisting arrest were released without bail. The four were required to post $150.00 bail.

The four students who were arrested while picketing for Kennedy at Rockefeller Center were represented by an attorney from the office of Assemblyman Jerome Kretchmer. One student was released because he was "under age," the attorney related, and the others were charged with disorderly conduct and obstructing pedestrian traffic.

The Coalition promises bigger and better demonstrations. "Each one will get progressively more militant," a spokesman said. "We think it's the healthiest development in the antiwar movement."

The spokesman explained that the split with the Fifth Avenue Coalition was "not in tactics as much as in the importance of taking an anti-imperialist line," but felt the tactics used Wednesday were effective. "The other tactics became necessary when we weren't allowed to picket," she explained. "We stayed on busy streets where we came into contact with a great number of people. Sometimes the cars that were stalled would beep their horns in time with the slogans. We saw a lot of support. If they were inconvenienced, they didn't seem to mind it."

Well, I saw a lot of drivers who were inconvenienced and did seem to mind, but you can't please everyone. Certainly the Beautiful People at the Diamond Ball didn't give a damn. It was a "Night of Nights," Doris Lilly wrote in the *Post*. "The grand ballroom was a bed of fragrant mimosa and red carnations. There was Meyer Davis's music and a Grade A dinner that featured a fish mousse, steak, and rivers of wine. The girls were given a gold pencil adorned with a diamond." It was, she said, "an event so brilliant as to be beyond description."

CHURCH OF THE STREETS

It would be easy to walk by the Washington Square Methodist Church a dozen times and never notice it. It's an ordinary church, with steps in front and a bulletin board to the side, and two steeples on top. The gray stone building stands flush with the apartment houses on West 4th Street off the southwest corner of the Square.

But last week the church was impossible to ignore. Scrawled across the ordinary wooden doors at the top of the steps, the white letters screamed: "A DEAD CHURCH CAN'T TALK!"

"The church doors have influence," said the Reverend A. Finley Schaef, minister of the church. "What might be ignored on a fence or a wall will be noticed on the doors of a church."

The doors are a new medium and the message is change. The change has been developing deep in the bowels of this Christian congregation for some time. It recently culminated in a statement adopted by the quarterly conference of the congregation—with no dissenting votes—which declared that "Washington Square Methodist Church is a Peace Church." The conference went on to declare that the church is "open" to peace groups, to direct the church treasurer to deduct the federal tax from the telephone bill as a protest to the Vietnam war, and to set up a service to find housing—in the church, if necessary—for conscientious objectors and draft resisters.

The declaration seemed at once a formality and a threshold. Last week it was announced that the Greenwich Village Peace Center would move from its present headquarters on Sheridan Square to a new office in the basement of the church. In an adjoining room, the Bread and Puppet Theatre has been giving performances for several months. And six members of the congregation are enrolled in draft-counseling courses.

Schaef welcomed the Peace Center to the peace church. "The people at the Peace Center are the peacemakers whom Christ called blessed," he said in the announcement of the move. "They not only belong in the church. They are the church—witnessing, acting, talking, demonstrating, vigiling, counseling, helping, protesting, writing, cajoling, and persuading—right out in the front, a prayer on feet, goading the conscience, never letting us forget that war is death."

And he welcomes the draft resisters. "We are the ones who are lying by the roadside and they are the good Samaritans."

The change in the church was gradual and almost organic. Last spring, Schaef recalled, the congregation began to sing the last hymn of the service outside on the steps. "The church belongs in the streets," he said. "Life has to be humanized in the city. We think of ourselves as a street church."

On Christmas Eve, the church had a street celebration. The congregation walked in a large circle around the Village, some in costumes, others with banners and balloons. And the last time the church took in new members, the ceremony was held by the fountain in Washington Square. After the ceremony, they danced around the fountain. "We danced to celebrate the new strength," Schaef explained. "Every new member makes us stronger.

"We're trying to say that life can still be celebrated," he went on. "It's still in our hands. I think that's the essence of the Gospel. However hard times get, it's still our life. We're not victims."

The peace mission of the church was developed in the winter. "Our worship study group met weekly trying to decide the right way to worship," Schaef recalled. "We decided that it was blasphemous to worship in isolation. We decided that peace was where our hearts were. So we went to the Whitehall demonstration."

In February the church took to the street again, to circle the Village carrying a huge homemade icon and a seven-foot cross "in silent witness and judgment" of the war in Vietnam.

And now the church will house draft resisters and the Peace Center. "We'd like to develop the idea of a sanctuary," Schaef said. "It's a difficult notion to work with because it doesn't have the substance it used to. It's not a literal type of thing where you can keep out the police but a moral type of thing where we can lend our help."

The refreshing thing about the change in the Washington Square Methodist Church is that it seems free of the deadening, self-conscious liberalism that so often is the offspring of a marriage between piety and politics. Too many attempts to move from an old form to a new form have been stalled by caution in the festering limbo of a middle form. With conscience braced against compromise, with the determination and instinct that comes from a deep well of faith, the church seems to have vaulted this morass. The atmosphere is now liberated.

"What we've done is not enough," Schaef said. "It's a beginning step which everyone knows involves much more than Vietnam. It's a revolution in our hearts. I think we're waking up to a dark and grisly past. Those skeletons they dug up on the Arkansas prison farm symbolize that for me. We have to wake up, repent, and change. The first sermon Jesus gave was repent. The problem of the church is that we still repent in sermons. Repent is an active verb —to turn about.

"Andy Young of the Southern Christian Leadership Conference said, 'If you take one step, the Lord will take the next two.' It's always happening."

The white letters are gone now and, for the meantime, the church doors are just doors again. The passerby still might not notice the ordinary church on West 4th Street but perhaps he will feel it.

THE RIGHT OF SANCTUARY

Don Baty burned his draft card with seventy-five other men in the Sheep Meadow in Central Park on April 15, 1967. He dropped out of college the next day to work full time for peace. His draft board sent him several duplicates, which he burned or returned, and ordered him three times to take preinduction physicals, which he refused to do. During the following year, he was arrested seven times for peace activities. On March 4, Baty refused induction at Fort Hamilton in Brooklyn. He was indicted, and was to be arraigned last Friday in Federal Court in Brooklyn. That morning, Don Baty sat with one hundred friends on the steps of the altar at the Washington Square United Methodist Church.

While there was never any question about the legal force of religious sanctuary, the symbolic power of the medieval ritual seemed to be a potent means of communicating what Baty, the church, and his friends felt was a "moral confrontation" with the government over the draft and the war in Vietnam. It had been tried only once before, several weeks ago, when a last-ditch draft resister and an AWOL Vietnam veteran were granted sanctuary in the Arlington Street Church in Boston. The resister was dragged out of the church by Federal marshals the next day; the AWOL veteran remained for a week. There should be many instances of sanctuary over the next year. Now that church congregations are ready to grant such support, resisters are ready to accept it. It is a way of saying to the government: "Now step over this line."

The morning began with a press conference. The pews had been moved back and to the side and Baty, his mother, and the Reverend A. Finley Schaef, the minister of the church, sat at a table in front of the altar. Schaef began by explaining how Baty had asked for sanctuary a week before and said that the congregation and the governing board of the church, in accordance with a policy established earlier in the year, had voted to grant him sanctuary. "The right of sanctuary in the Middle Ages was a right of impunity to crime," he said. "It was also a shield of innocence. This church, in granting sanctuary to Don Baty, is not granting impunity to crime, but rather is declaring his innocence. He has committed no crime in refusing by conscience to kill."

Then Baty read his statement. He refused induction, he said, "because I feel that the Vietnamese war, all war, is a senseless waste of life." He recounted his resistance to the draft over the last year, and said that he would refuse counsel and defend himself against charges of refusing induction. "As long as the United States Government continues to wage this unjust war against the people of Vietnam," he said, "the only place for a man to be is in jail." He said that he was "not taking sanctuary to avoid arrest. . . . I take sanctuary in order to make clear the moral issues I was raising when I refused induction."

Don Baty, when considering the public image of peaceniks and draft dodgers, was almost too good to be real. Although he is twenty-two, he looks seventeen, and his short, neat blond hair, beardless face, white shirt, and corduroy jacket could soothe the most alienated mother. After reading his statement, he went on to talk about peace and love and the waste of war. Shy but determined, his sincerity was disarming. The clichés came from the bottom of his heart.

His mother, Mrs. William Storey of Delmar, New York, spoke next to the press. Like her son, she was perfect: tidy, with glasses and nice dress and gray hair. She seemed tense, but determined to stand by her son.

"One of the questions I'm often asked," she began, "is, Are you proud of your son? Yes, I'm proud of my son, but I have no right to be proud of him, because it is he, not I, who is committed.

"Don is eligible many times over to be a member of the Sons of the American Revolution. He was brought up in a home where a musket used in the Battle of Breed's Hill hung over the fireplace. When he asked about these matters as he was growing up, we explained them carefully. We emphasized the importance of freedom."

She spoke briefly about his youth, and said he had been a Boy Scout. "As a Scout, Don was taught to work for God and his country. I believe what Don is doing is best for God and country."

Mrs. Storey finished by saying she sometimes felt that young people today were taking literally all the American ideals they had been taught to believe. "It is not surprising that Don is here today considering the spoken ideals of our generation."

After the formal press conference, Don Baty and his mother went outside to be interviewed by three network television news teams, who had refused to come into the church. And the real confrontation was packaged in videotape to be laid before how many million Americans who think they know America, whose duty is to judge.

No one knew when the warrant would be issued for Baty's arrest, or when the marshals would come to take him away. No one knew how the marshals would respond to the lines of supporters around Baty and the altar, or whether they would be violent, but everyone talked about it and tried to get together. "We have agreed not to impede the arrest," a girl stood up and said. "But we won't move. We'll let the marshals step over our bodies. A lot of us, including girls, will say 'I am Don Baty' when they ask for him. . . . This is intended as a show of solidarity, and not an impediment.

Then they rehearsed it, and everyone sitting round the altar said "I am Don Baty" in unison.

Baty emphasized again that he wanted the demonstration to be entirely nonviolent. "A lot of things are going to be swinging around in their heads when they come into church to bust," he said, "so don't even feel violent."

Vintone Ziegeler, the chairman of the church board, came in with the first media reports. He paraphrased the report on CBS radio, and the kids were pleased.

Then Schaef brought bread and wine to share in symbolic communion with the people in the church.

At 12:10 p.m. the word came that the warrant had been issued, and the people gathered in three tiers around the altar and sang "We Shall Overcome." The pews had been moved to the side of the church, leaving wide empty space between the hundred people packed around the altar and the doors through which the marshals would enter. Baty suggested a few minutes of meditation, and the church fell silent. . . . The noon sun streamed through the stained-glass windows. Schaef stood in the center of the room, facing the altar, holding a small child by the hand.

Still no marshals, and the people relaxed, and began to talk. Suddenly an older man walked into the church and up to the altar, and began to warn the people that what they were doing was interfering with and resisting Federal marshals, which could be a serious Federal offense. Media swarmed around him. Kids, at first stunned, began to shout him down. Schaef rushed to his side.

He turned out to be E. L. Million, professor of law at NYU, vice-president of the board of trustees of the church, and a member for twelve years. He wore an

American flag pin in his lapel, and he had led the minority faction in the church board who had opposed the granting of sanctuary. He said that he came to warn the kids that they might get into trouble. "I wanted to make sure they were not misled. There's no question that it's an illegal act." He argued with Schaef. "One of the objections I had was that you prostituted the church to politics," he said. He was upset that the kids were leaning against the altar, and at the word "desecration" he was invited outside to talk to the television cameras. Schaef followed, and they were taping for ten minutes. "I oppose the idea of a performance of a charade in the sanctuary," Million said. "To my mind, the sanctuary is made holy by such action," Schaef replied.

Million left and the marshals arrived, six heavy marshals in a dark brown truck. Schaef met the marshals before the altar. "Myself, my wife, and the people gathered here would like to declare the innocence of Don Baty," he said. "We are here because we suffer daily the horror in Vietnam. We do not feel that he is guilty under the law of God, nor under the laws of this land."

Schaef stepped aside and the marshals, who had a photograph, climbed quickly over the people and grabbed Don Baty. Baty went limp, and they pulled him down over the people, Baty with his fingers in a V, and they carried him out of the church through a crush of press to the van outside. The supporters followed, all hands in V's, to see the marshals hustle Baty into the van and leave.

About seventy-five people from the church followed Baty to the Federal Court Building in Brooklyn, where he was to be arraigned. The marshals carried Baty into the courtroom. He refused to stand while the charges against him were read, and Judge Joseph C. Zavatt cited him for contempt. Baty refused counsel and bail, and the marshals carried him out of the courtroom. He was taken to the Federal House of Detention on West Street.

It was a drama that was highly reflective of the times. It was perfectly cast: a sterling American youth, who acted out the ideals that have become clichés through lip service; the loyal American mother, who saw the future in her son; the bearded young minister, who believed such commitment holy; the elderly church layman, who believed such charades were sacrilege; the heavy, tense marshals who were doing their job; the angry judge, wary of contempt and the press.

It was also a drama designed to be channeled through the news media, so carefully staged that the participants were in a sense actors, so that nothing seemed quite real. The medieval ritual of sanctuary seemed appropriate not only because of the moral issues involved, but also as a ritual per se, like draft-card burnings and induction-center solidarity, and old ritual resurrected as a new ritual, tailored for the media, another gut symbol in the constantly escalating struggle to communicate the agony of the war and its effects.

RUN FOR THE EXIT

It must have been, for many New York liberals, a tantalizing opportunity to support the Black Panthers (all

the more appealing for their recent alliance with the
Peace and Freedom Party), to watch the Black Panthers
(let alone Marlon Brando and H. Rap Brown) do their
thing, and to recharge the old Black Power batteries, a
little drained after a long Vietnam winter and a heavy
spring. The whites turned out in droves at the Fillmore
East Monday night for a benefit to raise bail for jailed
Panthers Eldridge Cleaver and six brothers in Oakland.
Blacks came, too, maybe to watch the whites, and the
resulting crush around the box office was almost a utopian
gray.

The benefit had been sold out, but it still took almost
two hours to get the tickets sorted and everyone inside.
There, estrangement set in; with a little help from the
stage, black remained black and white became pale, at
best, or pink. The agony must have been exquisite for
those who remained beyond the crumbling of aesthetics.
Many left, and the remaining white audience got
whupped—in at least one case literally—when a white
man, overcome early in an incredibly long and tedious
rap in the dark by LeRoi Jones in his own play *Home on
the Range* (which was to leave gaping blocks of vacant
seats and a smoke-filled lobby), stood to protest "Bullshit!
Bullshit!" and was smoothly hustled into the lobby by im-
promptu bodyguards, laid up against the wall, and
knocked around, New York City plainclothesman style,
before being kicked out into the street. With due respect.

Brando didn't show, nor did H. Rap Brown. But LeRoi
Jones got the show rolling, flashing on stage with a Mus-
lim greeting and Arab messages of good will. And five
bodyguards. "I'm neither crazy nor mad nor any of these
things," he said with vigor. "It's just that many people
don't accept the truth of what I say. We want the power

to govern our lives," he continued. "We want to say what is beautiful for us. If you dig Campbell Soup cans, if you dig the American flag, if you dig imitating black men, you can do that. But we don't want to do that."

The playwright went on into a rap on the six-thousand-year black heritage and the three-hundred-year American history.

"We know that we are the masters and you are the slaves," he said. "We know that you still revere us. We know that you still imitate us. We know that you still need us around so you can suck our blood."

Jones talked about the school boycott in Newark. "We're boycotting the schools so children can learn about themselves.

"We do not want them to grow up to be Marlon Brando.

"We do not want them to grow up to paint Campbell Soup cans.

"We do not want them to grow up to think that somehow the celebration of homosexuality is aesthetic and profound.

"We are the creators; you white people are the imitators. There is no such thing as integration when one is the master and one is the slave.

"The same people who killed Bobby Hutton," Jones said later, "the same people who jailed Rap Brown, are the same white people who are sitting in this room."

Cheers and whistles. At the end, applause.

It was billed as an evening of Black Theatre, and there were four one-act plays. The first, which followed Jones, was *How Do You Do?* a play by Ed Bullins performed by the Black Troupe of Harlem. *How Do You Do?* has a brother-narrator-observer who is thinking about doing a

song when he gets distracted by an utterly bourgeois
satiated bleached black couple who court by reciting lux-
uries. It had the clarity and exaggeration of a contempo-
rary Chinese (political) opera of the absurd. Another
play, by Enrique Vargas's Gut Theatre of Harlem, had a
cop trying to get some Puerto Ricans to help him catch a
Negro, and they all ganged up on him and sprayed him
with his own Mace.

The Theatre Black ensemble from Cleveland performed a dramatized poetry reading called *Ghetto
Sounds,* which evolved from moping and bitching around
to a crescendo of flaming rhetoric, a riot in the aisles, and
spit flying around the orchestra seats. And Jones's monot-
onous rap in *Home on the Range,* the last play, finally
gave way to a scene with a family in whiteface, actually
grotesque flesh-colored rubber masks, who totally freaked
and disintegrated into the gibberish from whence he had
them spring when a black brother walked in with a gun.

Everyone liked Mrs. Eldridge (Kathleen) Cleaver, who
is running for State Senator on the Peace and Freedom
Party ticket in California. She described the police
("pigs") attacks on the Panthers in Oakland, particularly
the encounter on April 6 in which Panther Bobby Hutton
was killed, her husband wounded and now, with six
others, in jail. She described the coalition between the
Panthers, SNCC, and the Peace and Freedom Party, sug-
gesting that it was "proper for the revolutionary forces in
the colony to work with the same forces in the mother
country working to destroy the same structure." She was
followed by James Forman, who made a heavy pitch for
bread.

The lights went on. "There are brothers coming around
with baskets," Forman said, "and I'll talk. We intend to

collect two or three thousand dollars from this audience."
Forman went on to tell a story about how the rice growers
in Vietnam give so much rice to the Vietcong, but if it's
not enough, the Vietcong set up checkpoints and take
what they need. "If we don't get this three thousand
dollars," he said, "we'll have to set up a checkpoint, just
like the Vietnamese. Give up those dollars willingly. We
don't want to have to extract them. Let's see some bills.
Not just nickels and dimes. Let's see some fives." The
brothers moved around with the baskets, and they slowly
filled.

"Is there anyone who has not voluntarily given his
contribution?" Forman asked a little later, looking around
the Fillmore's 2,621 seats. "We don't want to set up a
checkpoint as you go out tonight after Bobby Seale has
finished speaking."

Apparently satisfied, Forman read some announce-
ments. "Here's one," he said, "and I'm just going to read
part of it first. 'City Human Rights Commissioner William
Booth will speak. . . .' "

Boos and hisses.

"That's what I figured," Forman said.

Bobby Seale, chairman of the Black Panther Party,
came on last, accompanied by four bodyguards. "It's
Monday night," he mused, "and Monday night, Tuesday
night, Wednesday night, Thursday night, Friday night,
Saturday night, and Sunday night and the pigs occupy
our community like foreign troops. Every day, every
night, every week, every year." This, he said, is what
colonization of black people in the confines of America is
all about.

Seale explained that the Black Panther Party was not
purely militaristic, although they urge black people to

arm for self-defense. He emphasized the ten-point program of the Black Panther Party. And he talked about Black Power.

"Power," he said, "is the ability to define phenomena and make it act in a desired manner. . . . In Mississippi and in Harlem, black people don't have black power. In San Francisco, in Detroit, in Chicago, in all those cities you heard about, black people don't have black power. . . . We must be able to make that pig act in that desired manner."

Gun power is real power, Seale said. "Organized guns and force in the black community are so necessary it's a crying shame.

"We hate you white people!" he shouted. "We hate you white people! And the next time one of you paddies comes up here and accuses me of hating you because of the color of your skin, I will kick you in your ass. We started out hating you because of the color of your skin. . . .

"The brothers are getting hip," he said. "The brothers are getting hip on the block, they're getting very, very hip. Five years ago no one knew anything about Molotov cocktails. Now thousands of brothers know what they are, how to make them, when to use them, and where to throw them.

"Huey P. Newton was into educating people on the right tactics. He'll tell you in a minute that spontaneous riot is bad tactics. We're going to use tactics they can't use. That's what the Vietnamese do. One gun can get you ten guns. That's what the Vietnamese do. Black people will parallel it quickly. . . .

"What the black brother wants is a program to be able to deal with the system. . . .

" 'How can he get the land and the bread?' Frantz Fanon.

"White people!" Seale screamed. "You! You liberal, you are like this to me: in school, when a little white liberal walked by I used to come up with my knife and say, 'Give me your lunch money or I'll cut your guts out!' And he'd give me his lunch money. Pretty soon I'd say, 'Tomorrow you bring me two dollars.' And the next day he'd bring me two dollars. Because that two dollars was mine. Mine because of four hundred years of racism and oppression. When I take two dollars from you, pig, don't you say nothing.

"Liberals, you are in this position, and you can just go and tell the principal, because the principal can't do nothing any more. Liberals, I'm going to force you to support the black liberation movement.

"We are talking about black revolution. We are talking about bloody black revolution. If you shoot at us, we're gonna shoot back, and if you look like you're gonna shoot, I'm gonna shoot first. So liberals, get off your rumps. . . . We're going to use as many of you people—you white people—as we can to destroy your racist system."

Seale spoke for about forty-five minutes and then, suddenly, he and his bodyguards were gone. The house lights were on—he wanted it that way—and Forman came out and said that H. Rap Brown was in New Orleans and Marlon Brando was somewhere else and thank you and good night. The theater emptied quickly, many out the side doors, many through the lobby where, sadly, there were no checkpoints. The Panthers must have been satisfied.

The least you can say about white skin is that it seems to be pretty thick.

LONG HOT SPRING

Henry is a new hero on the Lower East Side. I have my doubts about Henry. I never met him and I'm told he's dead.

Three weeks ago, a scruffy band of East Side natives gathered in front of the Ninth Precinct station—"The Embassy" to natives—to protest the latest of a tediously long series of busts of the crash pads of their brothers and neighbors. A veteran student of the New York hippie might recall the early busts in that series that skyrocketed Galahad to fame. After the thirtieth bust, the New York Civil Liberties Union became interested and helped Galahad sue in Federal Court to enjoin the police from busting his pad—and any other pad—without a warrant. Groovy was a co-plaintiff. Now Groovy is dead and Galahad is gone and the suit is still pending and the busts are still coming.

So three weeks ago, after the cops busted a crash pad on 1st Street, without a warrant, and arrested eight people on narcotics charges, after which two had their paroles revoked, the kids confronted the cops. One kid scaled the wall of the Ninth Precinct and sat on the ledge of a second-story window and yelled down, "Hey, they got pin-ups in there." And some other kids demanded that the cops arrest them, too, like Galahad used to, and then suddenly a dozen kids split and ran toward Second Avenue and disappeared around the corner. A few minutes later they were back, with long, long faces.

"Henry is dead," they said, and the crowd groaned.

"The cops killed Henry," they said, and the crowd seethed, and a few minutes later the crowd left the cops behind and ran up Second Avenue, stopping traffic, dumping a little garbage, freaking St. Mark's Place, and bitching about their hard-luck brother Henry.

The kids weren't talking, and the cops didn't like it, because no police precinct in the City of New York is so conditioned to talking as is the Ninth. "We're always ready to talk," they say, and talk and talk and talk, but after the talk the busts go on and nothing has changed. It's all the same. So, sure as the equinox, two weeks ago Thursday the cops busted another crash pad, this time on 7th Street, without a warrant, and they found the two runaways they said they were looking for and busted seven people for dope while they were at it. The cops brought three patrol cars for the two runaways, and busted up the apartment, breaking things, and the kids got prison haircuts the first night in jail.

So a handbill appeared calling for a second confrontation, and a couple of hours later Deputy Inspector Joe Fink dropped by the ESSO office and wanted to, you guessed it, talk. ESSO was ready to talk, but ESSO is an open storefront which leads to a resident crew of winos, who usually crash peacefully on the floor, but who are instantly aroused at the sight of a cop, let alone a deputy inspector. So while Fink tried to talk, the winos climbed all over him, even tried to pick a fight, and Fink gave the high sign to the patrol car waiting up the block and it seemed for a moment that the confrontation might come sooner than was originally expected. But a clash was avoided, and the kids got ready to confront the Ninth Precinct later that night.

They started to gather on 5th Street around 8 p.m. a week ago Thursday night, and warmed up by moaning about Henry until their ranks had swelled to about one hundred and fifty. Then some firecrackers went off, and a few kids fucked around with spray paint on the sidewalk and some cars, and yelled, "Don't bust our crash pads" and "Henry lives!" A few older neighbors dumped some eggs on the kids, and the kids chased the neighbors, and the cops intervened, and so it went, back and forth, until the cops started to get up-tight. So the kids split to Second Avenue.

The kids ran up Second Avenue, not because anyone was chasing them, but because it was one of the first warm nights of spring and they were together. A half a block above St. Mark's Place, a picket line was circling in front of the Manhattan Democratic Club where, it turned out, Congressman Leonard Farbstein was about to speak. "Support our boys in Vietnam," the Lower East Side Mobilization for Peace Action (LEMPA) was chanting. "Bring them home now."

Suddenly they were overwhelmed by the sound of "Long hot summer!" and "Up against the wall, motherfucker!" as the kids rushed up the stairs to the second-story club where they were met by a barricade of angry Manhattan Democrats.

The police cleared the stairs and the kids ran down St. Mark's Place and the police began to arrive in numbers. The kids scattered, some crossing Third Avenue, others reversing to Second Avenue to run down 9th Street to reassemble at Cooper Square, where they gathered around to rock the Rosenthal sculpture until they realized it would wipe them out if it fell. Then, with the police still clearing St. Mark's Place, the kids ran west on 8th Street, jammed with evening traffic moving east.

It was weird to be in the West Village. It was like a sneaky Vietcong offensive, taking the revolution into the City on a warm spring night when the streets were clogged with tourists and the cops were unsuspecting. But it wasn't sneaky; it was spontaneous. The kids were exhilarated to be beyond the boundaries. Now they didn't know where they were going; they were just going ahead. They wove through the stalled traffic, pounding on cars. They called to the tourists to "Join the Revolution!" It was the revolution; the kids were shouting it to convince themselves.

The bystanders seemed dumfounded. They stood to one side, watching the kids go by like a parade. There was little reaction: a few smiled, a few cursed, but the kids didn't seem hostile, and perhaps the tourists were conditioned to expect anything in Greenwich Village. They might have been reassured by the absence of police, for there were no police now, except for a single patrol car trying to weave backward through the eastbound traffic to keep pace with the kids.

More police appeared as the kids turned south on Mac-Dougal Street, but they didn't try to stop the mob, which had now more than doubled in size. The kids surged past the park and down into the coffeehouse jungle where, dodging eggs coming down from the apartments, they were joined by a herd of teeny-boppers. They went east on Bleecker, north on Thompson, through Washington Square, and back on 8th Street to the East Side, where the

Tactical Patrol Force and men from two precincts were mustering a welcome.

The main thrust of the kids tried to get back to the Ninth Precinct, but the block was sealed off and a battery of cops was waiting at Second Avenue and 5th Street. There was a brief clash of cops and kids and the revolution scattered. For the next hour clusters of cops broke up clusters of kids standing on street corners up and down Second Avenue. The heat was on St. Mark's Place, where around 11 p.m. a force of about twenty TPF cops charged the kids standing around, nightsticks swinging, to clear the area. But, in the end, only a half-dozen arrests were made.

Ruben Martinez was arrested in front of the Fillmore East. The police contend that he threw a soda bottle, striking a patrolman, and state that they have five witnesses to the act. Martinez denies it, and also has witnesses. The police contend that they rescued Martinez from a group of neighbors who began to beat him up when they saw him throw the bottle. Martinez says that the cops beat him up.

What is indisputable is that Martinez has a broken arm, a fractured knee-cap, and two severe cuts in his head. I interviewed him, through a translator, the next day. Martinez, seventeen, a university student from Puerto Rico who is visiting New York, does not speak English.

Martinez said that he was attacked by the police after he had pointed out a plainclothesman. He said that police hit him on the head with nightsticks in the street. He said that after he was arrested and in the patrol car, he told the police that he didn't speak English, that he was from Puerto Rico, and they cursed him. While one policeman drove the car, he said, the other hit him with a nightstick, breaking his arm and knee-cap. He said that after he arrived at the Ninth Precinct station a policeman hit him in the mouth with a nightstick, loosening his teeth, while he was standing in front of the main desk. He said that in the Ninth Precinct station he signed lots of papers which were not translated into Spanish. He was then taken to Bellevue and treated for his injuries. He said that the doctor at Bellevue told the police that he shouldn't be moved, that he couldn't walk. Martinez said that the police indicated that if he couldn't walk, then they would drag him.

At midnight, about sixty kids returned to demonstrate in front of the Ninth Precinct. They carried a banner which read "LIBERTY, EQUALITY, FRATERNITY," and they were quickly dispersed.

The "revolution" was sparked by a tangible issue and, like a fire, went on to feed itself. The issues merge in the streets, and the streets become the issue. "Any demonstration in the streets is about everything," said a spokesman. "It's orgiastic." The heat and the temperature and the air and the dirt and your girlfriend in the hospital with hepatitis are all fuel for confrontation. In the spring, a catalyst may be needed; the busts suffice. In the summer, the kindling point may come of itself.

Nothing was happening the following Saturday except for a fantastic Doors concert at the Fillmore East. Nobody was into confrontation on Saturday, except for the cops. Tourists jammed St. Mark's Place and Doors fans crowded the block in front of the theater and the entire block in front of the Ninth Precinct was sealed off to contain three busloads of TPF cops and heavy riot equipment just in case.

The precaution may be the precipitation. It's hard for the structure to understand. Like Henry, it's a mystery.

YIP-IN AT GRAND CENTRAL

All the brass was watching. Chief Inspector Sanford Garelik, shielded by a cluster of Tactical Patrol Force heavies, leaned against the wall in the 42nd Street entrance to Grand Central Station, intently watching the churning sea of demonstrators. Sid Davidoff and Barry Gottehrer, Lindsay's roving sensory apparatus, roamed around the terminal for hours. And a dozen privileged persons of some sort lined the balcony above the escalators leading to the Pan Am Building, observing the melee below like Romans digging the arena.

All the brass was watching, and the cops were having a ball. "It was the most extraordinary display of unprovoked police brutality I've seen outside of Mississippi," Alan Levine, staff counsel for the New York Civil Liberties Union, said at a press conference on Saturday. "The police reacted enthusiastically to the prospect of being unleashed." Levine reported seeing several people forced to run a gauntlet of club-wielding cops while trying to flee from what has been characterized as a "police riot." Spitting invective through clenched teeth, cops hit women and kicked demonstrators who had fallen while trying to escape the flailing nightsticks. It was like a fire in a theater.

It was a Yip-In. "It's a spring mating service celebrating the equinox," read a Yippie handbill, "a back-scratching party, a roller-skating rink, a theater, with you, performer and audience." The Yip-In was held for Yippies to get acquainted, and to promote the Yippies' "Festival of Life," which will coincide with the Democratic National Convention in Chicago this summer.

The promotion was as heavy as the planning was weak. The Yip-In was announced at a press conference at the Americana Hotel, and several thousand handbills were distributed urging Yippies to come to Grand Central Station at midnight on Friday. Why Grand Central Station? "It's central, man," said one Yippie. How many Yippies would come? Well, it was a good way to test the pull of the media.

The media pull, and a lot of people came. Most came by subway, coming up out of the bowels of the 42nd Street station to fill the mammoth terminal like a diverted river might fill a dry lake. Soon it was a sea of heads, and it was hard to move. Balloons bounced above the crowd, as an estimated six thousand people were jammed together under the vaulted ceiling.

The crowd stirred and the balloons bounced for almost an hour, while the terminal continued to fill. Occasionally clusters of people took up chants, ranging from "Yippie!" to "Long Hot Summer!" to "Burn, Baby, Burn!" Shortly before one o'clock, kids began to climb to the roof of the information booth in the center of the terminal, where they began to lead the chants, and one militant climbed to the pinnacle of the information booth, striking a "Workers Arise!" pose, his fist raised in the air, and unfurled a banner which read, vertically, "UP AGAINST THE WALL, MOTHERFUCKER!" Two cherry bombs exploded, and the sound was greatly amplified in the huge room. Now the balconies were packed, and the cops were quivering in formation in the 42nd Street entrance.

There are four clocks on top of the information booth, and as the roof became more crowded the temptation to rape time apparently became irresistible. First kids turned the hands around, and then the hands suddenly disappeared.

I was standing close to the cops when they started to clear the entrance, shoving people into the terminal or out into the street, where more cops were waiting in formation. I ran around the corner to the Vanderbilt Avenue entrance, and came to the balcony that overlooked the terminal in time to see a wedge of blue slice into the crowd, nightsticks swinging, until they came to the information booth, where they paused. The kids slid off the roof and the crowd recoiled. The police surrounded the information booth and, in seconds, now reinforced, charged the crowd again, forcing the demonstrators back into the huge corridor which led to the subway. The crowd simply made a U-turn in a connecting corridor and flowed back into the terminal, and the cops went wild.

Now another formation of cops charged toward the stairs where I was standing, and I made for the street again, rounded the corner, and returned to the 42nd Street entrance, which was now entirely filled with police. I pinned on my press credentials and began to move through the police lines. My credentials were checked twice, and I was allowed to pass. At that point, I was stopped a third time by two uniformed cops. They looked at my credentials, cursed *The Voice,* grabbed my arms behind my back, and, joined by two others, rushed me back toward the street, deliberately ramming my head into the closed glass doors, which cracked with the impact. They dropped me in the street and disappeared. My face, and my press card, were covered with blood. I went to the hospital to get five stitches in my forehead.

So I missed the climax of the Yip-In, but I can pass on various accounts of witnesses. The police, it seems, continued to charge the crowd at random, first charging, always swinging the nightsticks, then pulling back, then charging again. Sometimes several formations of police charged simultaneously in different directions. The exits were jammed and the crowd was in a panic, desperately trying to avoid the nightsticks. The police kept charging.

During all this time, arrests were being made. Within two hours fifty-seven persons were arrested, on charges ranging from felonious assault and criminal mischief to resisting arrest and disorderly conduct. At least twenty persons were taken to hospitals for treatment.

The arrest procedure followed a brutal pattern. Most of the people arrested were automatically beaten with nightsticks. (The cops didn't seem to want anyone to walk out after having been arrested.) "If you protected yourself, you were resisting arrest," a witness said. "If you didn't, you were knocked out." A youth was arrested near the escalator leading into the Pan Am Building, and was dragged across the terminal, screaming with pain, while police kicked him in the groin. He finally collapsed, and police grabbed him by the back of the belt, and carried him out to the waiting paddy wagons.

At another point, *Voice* columnist Howard Smith relates, the police made a charge toward the west side of the terminal, and a soda bottle came flying out of the crowd, striking a cop. Five cops grabbed a kid—the wrong one, Smith said—and shoved him into the door of Track 32, where they began beating him with nightsticks. While the kid, later identified as Jon Moore, seventeen, screamed "I didn't do it" and "It wasn't me," the crowd shouted "Sieg Heil!" Still the beating continued. Some other cops approached and tried to stop the beating, Smith said, and then a police captain approached and made the guise of breaking it up. Moore, who was now hunched over protecting his head and groin, looked up, and the captain grabbed his head and cracked it against the iron grating of the door, cursing "You son of a bitch." The captain then turned away, brushing his hands, and Moore was taken out of the station. He was later charged with felonious assault.

These incidents were not exceptional. Ronald Shea, twenty-two, was shoved by police through a plate-glass door. He raised his hands to protect his face, and the broken glass severed every essential tendon and nerve in his left hand. In six months, doctors at Roosevelt Hospital say, he may regain partial use of his hand. Shea was not arrested.

Witnesses charged that several plainclothesmen, who had infiltrated the crowd before the police charged, were even more brutal than the uniformed cops when the swinging started. They add that the plainclothesmen, who wore no badges, refused to identify themselves when questioned by accredited newsmen. Several instances were reported when cops struck or intimidated people seen writing down badge numbers. Witnesses emphasize that no warning or order to disperse was given at any time before or after the police charged the demonstrators, although a public-address system was presumably availa-

ble in the station. Ed Sanders of the Fugs contends that
the people would have responded to a warning. "People
who come to Yippie demonstrations are very reasonable,"
he said. "There was no reason to rush in and crunch."

After the police first charged, Abbie Hoffman, YIP
leader, reportedly approached Barry Gottehrer, assistant
to the mayor, and asked to use the terminal's public-
address system. Gottehrer replied that he thought Hoffman was "an hour and a half late" and refused. Hoffman
then asked that the police be pulled out, and Gottehrer
presumably refused again.

After an hour and a half, the cops calmed down, and
the remaining demonstrators were allowed to remain in
the terminal. Others went to the Sheep Meadow in Central Park, also staked out with police, where the organizers of the Yip-In had planned to meet to "yip up the
sun." By 4:15 a.m., Grand Central Station was empty.

Saturday morning the key leaders of YIP, Abbie Hoffman, Jerry Rubin, Paul Krassner, and Bob Fass, left New
York to fly to Chicago for a conference regarding the
planning of activities during the Democratic National
Convention. Later that morning, the fifty-seven people
arrested were arraigned in court. Most of the people were
represented by Legal Aid. YIP had made no arrange-
ments for lawyers or bail.

There was a lot of garbage and buck-passing flying
around during the following days. Gottehrer, at a YIP
press conference Sunday night, placed considerable emphasis on the crowd on top of the information booth, the
cherry bombs, and the damage to the clocks. He refused
to concede any misconduct on the part of the police. YIP
spokesmen complained about a breakdown of communications, insisting that they had never considered the pos-

sibility of violence. On Monday, the scuttlebutt at City Hall included rumors that some of the demonstrators were carrying dynamite Friday night, and privately city officials alleged that the police received two bomb threats at Grand Central Station. Now the rumors have gone even further, with representatives of both sides darkly referring to "provocateurs" who incited the police to riot.

As I see it, the central issue—besides the astonishing brutality of the police—was a failure in planning on the part of both YIP and the City that borders on gross incompetence and irresponsibility. Although YIP had been in contact with the mayor's office before the demonstration, the City gave no indication as to what their response would be. The City urged YIP to consult with the New York Central Railroad, which owns Grand Central Station, which YIP did not do. The demonstration was allowed to form without interference or objection and, an hour later, without warning, the police viciously attacked the crowd. There was little direction or coordination evident in the cops' attack; they seemed to be improvising. YIP did not even bring a megaphone so that they could address their own people; in the situation that developed, the leaders found themselves impotent.

The cardinal insanity was the selection of Grand Central Station for an enormously publicized demonstration of totally indeterminate size. The Yip-In was the fourth and by far the largest demonstration to be held at the terminal. The first three all ran into cops. It was a pointless confrontation in a box canyon, and somehow it seemed to be a prophecy of Chicago.

EPILOGUE

I will neither affirm nor deny our immortality.

To affirm is to feed the fears and excuses of those unwilling to live in the present.

To deny is to lose sight of the uncertainty of future moments, to again forget that what we do now can make all the difference.

It is September 9th 1969, more than a year after your death, I do not know where you are Don McNeill.

Are you a part of me, writing these words? And if so, of how many others?

After your funeral a bunch of us, I can't remember who, got together in an apartment on Third Street, rapping—not about the past, the present—and listening to music; and we really felt together, felt good, a Gestalt—like the scene in *Stranger* after Mike is killed—you were what held us together, how could we miss you? Of all of us, you most certainly were there.

Dear reader, you are free to choose: Is life a matter of biochemistry, or of consciousness?

Don McNeill and I were extremely close friends for fifteen months—as close as I have ever felt to anyone. We have not been close since his death. But perhaps because there is no longer any distance between us?

We could relax in each other's presence—often more than either of us, I think, could alone. I have missed that comfort.

We could speak and know the other heard. Energy flowed forth and back in almost frictionless, divine, easy communication—we learned much from ourselves in the presence of each other.

And I am the one who's inherited that knowledge. I'm left holding the bag. I must write epilogues.

This book is a collection of news stories written, over the course of two years, for *The Village Voice*. For deadline. And Don, the procrastinator, wrestled with these words to the very last moment, every time. It is hard to imagine Don writing without a deadline.

Making lists, maybe. Taking notes. Typing sentence fragments onto yellow paper. But *writing?* It was always too soon for that.

This book is arbitrary, a collection of East Village/hippie/new world news stories written by a young man for a weekly newspaper. If it is a good book—I suspect that it is—that is the reader's achievement, not Don's. Don's only interest was in the compassionate truth—the contribution that truth told in print could make to the growth of his world—and, yes, the well-turned phrase, he always enjoyed his words and sentences, conscious of the music he could set free. But I don't think he ever realized how much of himself he expressed, revealed, in his careful reporting.

This book is full of Don McNeill, alive, aware, briefly and totally conscious at a time of great excitement for the human species. It is important to note that Don was an adventurer, he spent as much energy and courage on psychedelic exploration as any American pioneer expended in hopes of expanding man's potential reach—an adventurer is a man who lives out his own desire to discover, to enjoy life, to be free. My best memory of Don is our acid trips.

This book is true to Don, and that's all we need to know. And that Don is now neither mortal nor immortal, and that you too, reader, are alive. This I affirm.

Paul Williams

A NOTE ABOUT THE AUTHOR

Don McNeill was born on December 21, 1944, in Tacoma, Washington. He graduated from high school in Juneau, Alaska, and attended college at the University of Washington in Seattle. He dropped out of school early in his senior year and went to New York, where he worked as a free-lance writer before becoming a staff writer for *The Village Voice* in September 1966. He was still working for the *Voice* when he accidentally drowned on August 10, 1968, while swimming in a lake near a cabin he had rented with friends in upstate New York. Later, it was learned he was being treated for a case of latent pneumonia.

Photo: Diane Dorr-Dorynek

CITADEL UNDERGROUND provides a voice
to writers whose ideas and styles veer
from convention. The series is
dedicated to bringing back into print
lost classics and to publishing new
works that explore pathbreaking and
iconoclastic personal, social, literary,
musical, consciousness, political,
dramatic and rhetorical styles.

For more information, please write to

CITADEL UNDERGROUND
Carol Publishing Group
600 Madison Avenue
New York, New York, 10022

Take Back Your Mind

CITADEL UNDERGROUND books are published for people eager to stretch their minds around new and dangerous ideas.

CITADEL UNDERGROUND provides a voice to writers whose ideas and styles veer from convention. The series is dedicated to bringing lost classics back into print and to publishing new works that explore pathbreaking and iconoclastic personal, social, literary, musical, consciousness, political, dramatic and rhetorical styles.

We'd like to stay in touch with you. If you'd like to hear more about our plans for CITADEL UNDERGROUND, please fill out this card and send it to us. We're eager to hear your comments and suggestions.

CITADEL UN **DERGROUND**

"Challenging Consensus Reality Since 1990"

Carol Publishing Group • 1-800-447-BOOK
Sales and Distribution Center • 120 Enterprise Avenue • Secaucus, NJ 07094

- -

Please keep me posted about Citadel Underground books!

Name (Please Print)_____

Address_____

_____

City_____ **State**_____ **Zip**_____

Title of this Book_____

Favorite Bookstores (and Locations)_____

Fax_____ **Electronic Mail Address**_____

_____

Comments_____

_____

_____

NO POSTAGE
NECESSARY
IF MAILED
IN THE
UNITED STATES

BUSINESS REPLY MAIL

FIRST CLASS   PERMIT NO. 111   SECAUCUS, N.J.

POSTAGE WILL BE PAID BY ADDRESSEE

CAROL PUBLISHING GROUP

120 ENTERPRISE AVENUE

SECAUCUS, N.J. 07094-9899